For More Free Dyslexia Re

Liz has also created a website **DyslexiaDaily**   ind
resources. On this website you will also find the world's first **Worldwide Directory of Learning Difficulty Service providers.**

From one parent and teacher to another you will soon realise that you are not alone in your quest to support your child or student.

What you will find on DyslexiaDaily.com

- Free articles
- Free Posters
- Books and reviews
- Teaching resources and aids
- Evidence based educational programs

- A community forum
- The latest research
- Teaching and learning strategies
- A news blog

What you will find on the Directory?
A world wide and ever growing list of dyslexia service providers in your local area with over 30 categories including:

Dyslexia assessors
Dyslexia associations
Dyslexia friendly schools
Support groups
Educational psychologists
Developmental pediatricians
Psychiatrists
Visual processing specialists
Auditory processing specialists
Teacher training services
Government dyslexia coordinators
Tutors
.....and lots, lots more

**Worldwide Learning Difficulties Directory
dyslexiadaily.com**

Helping
children
with dyslexia

21 super strategies to ensure your
child's success at school

Best Wishes

Liz Dunoon

Liz Dunoon

First Edition 2010
Second Edition 2015

National Library of Australia
Cataloguing-in-Publication entry:

Dunoon, Liz
Helping children with dyslexia : 21 super strategies
to ensure your child's success at school / Liz Dunoon.
2nd ed.
ISBN: 978-0-646-94059-5 (pbk.)

Dyslexia children--Education--Australia.

Dyslexia children.

Published by Transformation Trust
PO Box 2 Park Orchards, Victoria 3114 Australia
For further information email support@dyslexiadaily.com

Foreword by
Sir Richard Branson

The thing about being dyslexic is there is always something that you can do really well and something you cannot do so well. Often dyslexics exceed in the areas they are good at and what they have to do is make sure they find other people to compensate for what they are not good at.

I became a very good delegator, which meant surrounding myself with people that were better than me. A lot of dyslexics are good at dealing with people - motivating people, inspiring people. They shouldn't let the things they are bad at get them down.

In business, you soon realise that as long as you can add, subtract and multiply that's all you need to know and even if you can't do that you'll find someone who can. I ended up running the largest group of European companies and it wasn't until I was 50 years old that someone explained the difference between gross and net. They pulled out a piece of paper, drew a picture of the ocean, put a fishing net in it and said the fish in the net is your profit (i.e net profit) and the ocean represents your turnover. By showing me in that simple way, I finally grasped it!

One of the great things about being dyslexic is that it has helped me when marketing any of our companies. I always need to simplify things, and I think that by doing this many more people understand and connect with what we are saying. Simple and transparent are what all our companies try to be and I think this has helped with our success.

It is important as a dyslexic that you don't spend energy worrying about what you can't do – but instead figure out what you can do and make sure you do it well.

I truly believe that being dyslexic can be turned in to a blessing. Make the most of what you have!

Liz Dunoon

Praise for 'Helping Children With Dyslexia'

'Discover new solutions for children with dyslexia. Liz Dunoon's book, explains it simply, provides a comprehensive plan of action and will help to ensure a successful future for your child'.

Prof. John Stein, FRCP
World leading dyslexia expert, Chairman of The Dyslexia Research Trust,
Oxford University, UK

'A bible for every parent of a dyslexic child. For me this book confirms you can never give up on your child's education, only you can protect them. No one else is going to do that for you, especially those children who aren't getting the right support in school. *Helping Children With Dyslexia* confirms a lot I knew. It confirms to me how important it is never to rely on the School Education System. Too many qualified staff told me my son was doing fine. - Ha ha, how wrong they were. I know so many parents who believe what they are told and their beautiful children slip through the net. Good luck - I hope this book makes a difference for you. Not only a great read for a parent, but for those working with dyslexic children.'

Charlotte Brown
Chiswick, London U.K.

'Congratulations on your book. I have been able to read through it and it is excellent. The quotes throughout the book are succinct and inspiring and they highlight the key issues faced by parents and educators. I am sure it will prove to be an invaluable and indispensable resource for all parents and teachers.'

Dr Gavin Reid
Ph.D.,M.A. M.App. Svi, M.Ed., B.Ed, AMBDA, Assoc. F.B.P.S.
Author of twenty two books on learning difficulties. International independent educational psychologist with active consultancies in seven countries. Dyslexia assessor. Presented at over 800 conferences in 50 countries. External examiner to over 15 universities for PhD candidates and masters courses. Teacher and university lecturer and most importantly a parent. U.K.

DyslexiaDaily.com

'This book **Helping Children With Dyslexia** is written by a parent of a dyslexic child who is also a teacher. It contains a wealth of advice from personal experience, from investigations of other parents' experiences and from the experiences of dyslexic people. There is also technical material about the nature and origins of dyslexia, but if this is not of interest to you, you could just skip those parts because the wisdom in the rest of the work is invaluable to a parent struggling to help their dyslexic child. How to support your child, how to relate to teachers, how to choose the right school, when to consider repeating a year, as well as strategies to adopt - all this and more is there from one who has been there and done that. A really helpful book for parents - and teachers too for that matter!'

Dr. Paul Whiting
President, Specific Learning Difficulties Association, NSW
As seen on '60 Minutes'

'Liz Dunoon's book **Helping Children With Dyslexia** is a must read for every parent and child affected by dyslexia. It will allow them the opportunity to understand how they can help their child to succeed at school and reach for the stars. As a young adult, I was diagnosed with dyslexia. For me, this was just a label that helped explain the previous years of failure and frustration that I experienced while at school and the fact I dropped out early. In later years however, I discovered a few simple key strategies that allowed me to change my mindset and the way I managed my learning and this changed my life. I have since gone on to obtain a law degree with pass grades in the top 5% of the University. As a result, I have gone from high school drop out to top university scholar and successful entrepreneur.'

Andrew Grant
Leading International Marketing Entrepreneur and best-selling author
As seen on 'A Current Affair'

'Starting school was a confusing and bewildering time for our youngest son who struggled to learn to read. Being highly capable and intelligent, we had no idea why this was occurring or how to help him. Liz Dunoon's book **Helping Children With Dyslexia** gave us the knowledge and strategies we were seeking. He has advanced through his reading levels, now equals some of the top readers in his class and is happy and confident at school. We can't thank you enough.'

Ruth Rutch
Sunshine Coast, Queensland, Australia

'Identifying dyslexic traits, understanding the biological nature of dyslexia and having your child diagnosed as early as possible are the keys to improving your child's chances of success at school and in life. Liz Dunoon's book *Helping Children With Dyslexia* will give you the knowledge and the confidence to tackle your child's dyslexia head on.'

Dr. Silvia Paracchini
The Wellcome Trust Centre For Human Genetics, Oxford University, U.K.

'My son struggles daily to cope with dyslexia in a world of print. During his first term of prep we struggled helplessly as he pulled us into a new world we knew nothing about - a world where despite trying his most heart-breaking best there could still be a complete and devastating failure to learn. Despite many years of research and professional opinions, I can only marvel at the way Liz Dunoon has gathered together the 'essential mapbook' to help guide those entering my son's world. Not only are the signposts clear and the information easily accessible - the insight into those who have 'gone before' and their encouragement allows the sun to shine out from behind the alphabet.'

Dr Kathryn Law
Melbourne, Victoria, Australia

'For many years I have been trying to find ways to help and support my struggling son. He was not doing well at school and this resulted in angry outbursts of frustration and an ongoing lack of concentration and confidence. Liz Dunoon's book *Helping Children With Dyslexia* has given me the courage to address these issues and find solutions. My son now enjoys learning and is experiencing success at school.'

Jane Wilson
Brisbane, Queensland, Australia

'In this gem of a book, Liz Dunoon uses her empathy as the parent of children with dyslexia and her skills as a teacher to empower parents to rise up and advocate on behalf of their dyslexic children. *Helping Children With Dyslexia* is a book that aims to take the fear and worry out of parenting a child with dyslexia, replacing it with hope and optimism and ultimately success. You don't even have to read it, you can just listen.'

Tracey Stranger
Author of 'How To Overcome Stress Naturally'

'In my role as Irlen Regional Director and Director of the Irlen Dyslexia Centre Melbourne, I assess children and adults with Irlen Syndrome, a form of perceptual dyslexia. During the last seventeen years, I have had the privilege

DyslexiaDaily.com

of testing over 6000 intelligent individuals whose main difficulty is translating visual information into written text. It is often an emotional time when parents realise that their child has been struggling for legitimate reasons and when children realise that it is not their fault and they are not dumb or lazy after all. Liz Dunoon's book seeks to dispel much of that anxiety and turmoil through education and empowerment. I have been trying to find time to write a book like this for many years and I am certain that this book will be well used and passed around to friends and acquaintances for many years to come.'

Gloria Thomas,
Irlen Regional Director, Victoria, Tasmania and ACT

'As a child with dyslexia I found school frustrating and limiting. It was after leaving school early I began to discover where my real talents lay and developed a passion for photography. With a heightened sense of form, light and colour, my photographic skills have taken me to amazingly beautiful places and enabled me to photograph some of the world's most beautiful people. Liz Dunoon understands that at school dyslexia can create barriers, but she also wants parents to realise that dyslexia can provide incredible talents. Parents need to help their children to find these special talents and watch them flourish. Reading **Helping Children With Dyslexia** will help parents to begin this journey.'

Paul Jons,
Professional Photographer, Caloundra, Australia

'Parents who are actively engaged in the school community and volunteer their time to assist teachers and students in the classroom are an integral part of a school community. Liz Dunoon's book **Helping Children With Dyslexia** encourages parents to have an active role in the education of their children, working together with teachers who are striving to achieve positive educational outcomes for all of their students, including those with learning disabilities.'

Mr. Neil Sampson
Head of Primary School, Nambour Christian College, Nambour, QLD, Australia

'The seemingly intelligent child who struggles to learn at school because of dyslexia is a mystery to many. Liz Dunoon has written **Helping Children With Dyslexia** with the sole intention of educating parents and teachers and making a difference in the lives of these children. It is education which empowers and allows parents and their children to imagine a successful future.'

Steven Grbac,
Grade 4 Teacher, Melbourne, Australia

Thank you

It is with a great deal of thanks that I would like to acknowledge the following individuals who have willingly volunteered their time, their expertise and their passion to help me to write this book. By working together we may help a child with dyslexia, but we might just help thousands and this is my dream. I am honoured to be associated with you.

To my husband Andrew. You have proved to me time and time again that male stereotypes don't apply; a true team effort to manage our family, our children, our home and our lives. Your incredible love and support are always forthcoming and your absolute steadfast belief in me is unwavering. You hold me accountable and make me feel powerful. Thank you.

To my three children. You are divine in the true sense of the word. I hope some day when the time is right you will read this book and be as proud of me as I am of you. The world is your oyster and you are the pearls.

You don't think I did this all by myself do you? The following represents a list of people who have contributed to this book on many levels and they need to be acknowledged.

Sir Richard Branson, Prof. John Stein together with his colleagues at The Dyslexia Research Trust, Oxford University. U.K. Dr. Silvia Paracchini , Prof. Anthony Monaco together with their colleagues at The Wellcome Trust Centre For Human Genetics, Oxford, U.K. Dr. Paul Whiting, Dr. Gavin Reid, Prof. Linda Siegal, Margaret Hardy, Gloria Thomas, Fiona Baudinette, Libby Barnes, Prof. Max Coltheart, Dr. Alex Richardson, Dr. Sue Fowler, Dr. Tom Scerri, Dr. Simon Fisher, Dr. Clyde Francks, Dr. Megan Dennis, Dr. Antonio Velayos, Dr. Clotilde Levecque Dr. Lawrence MacPhie, Dr. Janet Walter, Dr. Patricia Riddell, Dr. Piers Cornelissen, Dr. Peter Hansen, Dr. Ken McAnally, Dr. Joel Talcott, Dr. Catherine Stoodley, Dr. Joe Taylor, Darren Stephens, Andrew & Daryl Grant, Jo Munro, Tommy & Allison Rando, Joscelyn & Neil Howard, Lynne and David Dunoon, Steven Grbac, Ruth Rutch, Neil Sampson, Paul Jons, Stacy Peterson, Joanne Howard, Jason Cottam, Cindy Newbold, Nicole Ferrari, Leanne Dulei, Sharon & Andrew Cooper, Dr. Kathy Law, Clarice Davies, Kathy Campbell and Tracey Stranger.

To all the parents, grandparents, educators and carers. You willingly told me your stories, your concerns, your worries and your needs. You are the people who gave me the questions that needed answers and inspired me to find the solutions.

And we must also pay tribute to every parent who is prepared to choose the path of education to support their child with dyslexia, every educator who ever believed in, inspired and taught a child with dyslexia and every adult who stood up and publicly acknowledged having dyslexia and in doing so inspired others to overcome obstacles and succeed.

DyslexiaDaily.com

Contents

AUTHOR'S INTRODUCTION   XIII

CHAPTER 1:   1
Is my child dyslexic? I think they might be. How can I tell?

CHAPTER 2:   17
My child is showing some of the dyslexic characteristics. What do I do now?

CHAPTER 3:   25
How to get an accurate diagnosis for your struggling child

CHAPTER 4:   41
So what is dyslexia and how do you get it?

CHAPTER 5:   55
Dyslexia research - a simple explanation

CHAPTER 6:   69
My child is dyslexic. How does it feel to be dyslexic?

CHAPTER 7:   81
Are you ready for the dyslexia challenge?

CHAPTER 8:   97
My child has been diagnosed with dyslexia. Should I tell them and label them?

CHAPTER 9:   115
Shouldn't my child's teacher be able to tell me that my child is struggling to learn and may require testing for dyslexia?

CHAPTER 10:   133
Why school is so difficult for so many dyslexic children

CHAPTER 11:   141
How can I help my child with dyslexia and make their life easier at school?

CHAPTER 12:   159
How to decide if your child should repeat a year or change schools

CHAPTER 13:   169
I've heard about coloured glasses. How can I tell if they may help my child?

CHAPTER 14:   183
So what causes visual dyslexia and what can be done about it?

CHAPTER 15:   197
The psychological effects of struggling at school

CHAPTER 16:   207
How to put a support system in place for your child with dyslexia

CHAPTER 17:   215
How can I help my child to regain their confidence when they are already struggling at school and feel dumb and stupid?

CHAPTER 18:   227
A resource list you need to know about

CHAPTER 19   231
How to create an action plan

Introduction By The Author

I am just like you, the parent of a dyslexic child. I am constantly seeking ways to help my children succeed. If researching to write a book makes me an expert on dyslexia, then you can become one too. I am sure you and your family have an amazing personal dyslexic story worthy of being told.

I have a dyslexic, but extremely clever husband, Andrew. I also have three beautiful children with varying degrees of dyslexia. Because of this, I have been surrounded by dyslexics for a total of 22 years now. It was through my research into how to help my children that I discovered a lack of understanding and resources to assist me. I could see the pain, the confusion and the frustration that dyslexia was causing my children and I wanted it to stop straight away. Not next week, not in a month or a year's time, but right now. That is without shelling out thousands of dollars for tutors or to purchase resources and programs that I had no guarantee would work. Fear and guilt can make us pull out our wallets out of sheer desperation when our child is unhappy and struggling at school.

The more I looked, researched and spoke to teachers, the more I realised that there is a cavernous divide, almost as huge as the Grand Canyon, between what we know about dyslexia and how to treat it and what is available in the majority of our children's schools. This realisation, that so many dyslexic children were being ignored or were not being offered the appropriate support, spurred me into action. So much ignorance still exists and as a result there are many struggling and anxious dyslexic children in our schools trying to survive the day. Maybe your child falls into this category. If so, this book is for you.

Many years ago, I trained as a primary school teacher and worked in two very different schools. The first was a government school in a poor county town, where a student's basic needs of breakfast, sleep and emotional care were often a priority over teaching and learning. The students' behaviour in this school was extremely challenging and invariably got in the way of both teaching and learning.

The second school was an elite private school with excellent academic standards. My well behaved young students thrived in a resource rich classroom. In this school, all the teachers were made fully accountable for their students' success and teachers were provided with enormous levels of support. In this school it was rare for a child to fall behind academically.

As a teacher, I am proud to say that I never gave up on any of my students. I always strived to find a way to reach them and to help them learn, even though I had no real knowledge of learning disabilities. I wasn't yet married at that time and didn't have my own children. My determination was inbuilt and being a self-confessed perfectionist; I saw my students' failure to learn as my own personal failure.

I have the same ethos as a parent; I believe my children have the right to learn at school, to be happy and successful. To me, the fact that they have dyslexia should not be a major hurdle, but yet this continued to be the case. So I decided to find ways to guarantee my childrens' future happiness and their success. Like many parents today, I work and am time poor, so I researched and developed methods to help my dyslexic children that were fast, effective and enjoyable.

Being a past teacher I am not intimidated by my childrens' teachers or by the system and neither should you be. Many teachers and schools are falling way behind when it comes to understanding, supporting and teaching dyslexic children. While this continues to be the case, you must step up and take control of your child's destiny. Your child needs you. Parents are the key to their dyslexic child's future happiness and success.

Knowing what I know now, I understand that there continues to be many challenges facing teachers in today's society. One of these is a lack of ongoing training in teaching children with learning disabilities. Because of this, there are also many struggling dyslexic children receiving little or no support. I believe it is time for change and decided to write this book for dedicated parents who are determined to make a difference in the lives of their children.

In this book, I will give you answers to many of your questions and provide you with numerous strategies to help your dyslexic child to learn, be happy and succeed. You are the difference in changing what appears to be a hopeless situation for your child into one of understanding and education that leads to success.

The inspiration for this book has come from my family and the many dyslexic children and their parents who pass in and out of my life. They are the ones who continually strive to find a way forward to help their children to reach their goals and to realise their dreams. You can do this too.

This book is also about providing hope for the future. There are many amazing, inspirational, selfless academics working hard to demystify dyslexia. This includes scientists, psychologists, medical specialists, educators and campaigners who work tirelessly studying dyslexia and trying to educate the decision makers and power brokers as to what is possible by today's standards. If you as a parent want to continue to know the latest, then this book will show you how to go straight to the source. These research studies and reports are revolutionising how we identify, treat and teach dyslexic children. This book is a tribute to this groundbreaking research and for the hope it provides to every dyslexic child and to the parents who love and support them. On behalf of every family touched by dyslexia, I want to thank them for the contribution they are making to the lives of future generations.

Parents, here is your chance to begin an education that could change the life of your dyslexic child forever. I have decided to change the way the world views dyslexia and share with you how to enrich the life of your beautiful dyslexic child. I hope you enjoy the journey to a happier more successful place.

Start reading at the place that suits you and your child best.

Happy reading or if you prefer you can just listen.

Liz Dunoon

Chapter 1

Is my child dyslexic?
I think they might be.
How can I tell?

Is My Child Dyslexic?

If you are asking yourself this question, you are probably wondering whether your child has a learning difficulty, a learning disability or maybe even dyslexia. Maybe you have been told that they have dyslexia, but you are still not sure what this means and need to know more. Maybe you also struggled to learn at school and are recognising some worrying similarities in your own child.

As mothers, fathers and the primary carers of children, we may have a sense that our child is not developing at the same rate as others and that things may not be progressing as well as we would like. Maybe a teacher or knowing friend has indicated that your child may have dyslexia. Once you have ruled out poor eyesight and hearing via a qualified medical doctor, it is time to investigate further.

The uncertainty of not knowing whether your child has a learning disability can cause parents inner turmoil and conflict. We desperately want our children to be perfect in every way and will provide every opportunity for them to prove that they are. At this point you need to be congratulated, because you are overcoming a natural parental tendency to want to protect your child and cushion them from the harsh realities of life. The time you take to do this is critical to a child with a learning disability. Early intervention is always best.

Look at it like this; by reading this book you are ensuring you are well informed. If dyslexia or a learning disability is affecting your child, the earlier you know about it, the better. This is because your knowledge is the key to your child's success at school and in life.

Please be aware that having dyslexia is not an indication of lower intelligence. Research studies indicate that people with dyslexia are generally of equal or higher intelligence when compared to the general population. One of the greatest barriers for children with dyslexia is formal academic schooling. This is why it is so important for parents to be aware of how the school system will impact upon their child with dyslexia. With your unconditional love, ongoing education and support, your child can be successful throughout their school years and throughout their life.

Why Parents Are The Key To Their Child's Success

Your child with dyslexia needs you more than ever to get through their years of formal schooling. Once you begin to assist them, their confidence will begin to increase; your child will begin to shine and you will see a noticeable difference in them. There are no quick fixes for children with dyslexia. You are beginning a journey, but it will mean a great deal to your child to know that you understand their plight, believe in them and will advocate on their behalf. With your help, your child will have the opportunity to reach their full potential, and isn't that what we all want for our children?

"When your child started school it was never their intention to struggle and fail; only to succeed and make you proud."

How Many People Have Dyslexia?

The statistics vary slightly from study to study, but the latest research indicates that as many as 10% of people in developed English speaking countries worldwide may be affected by dyslexia. That figure represents approximately 1 in every 10 people. Dyslexia can range from very mild to extremely severe and no two people will ever exhibit exactly the same symptoms, even when they come from the same biological family.

Why Boys And Girls Exhibit Learning Difficulties Differently

Is your child a boy or a girl and does it really matter? At this point do you need to consider the sex of your struggling learner? There has been a long held belief that boys are affected more regularly with dyslexia. However studies in this area are contradictory in their findings. You need to consider the fact that it may be possible that there are equal numbers. Boys tend to be more outwardly vocal and misbehave when they are having difficulty learning. As a result, more boys may be referred to specialists. Girls can go unnoticed; they are in general more controlled and not as vocal. A difficulty with learning can become harder to observe in girls as they can withdraw, and put in a big effort to try to hide their feelings and their difficulties. Some girls will even try to work harder to overcome their learning problems. They may be aware of their differences and try to overcome them through sheer effort and hard work.

Maryanne's Story

Maryanne's 9 year old son Max was having learning difficulties at school. She decided to take him for an educational assessment at a local clinic. Max was being shown a range of cards upon which text had been altered to represent what he might see if he was perhaps visually dyslexic. He was also asked if when he was reading the words ever jumped around on the page. Maryanne became uncomfortable as she looked over his shoulder. 'Doesn't everybody see words like that?' she asked, 'Don't the words always move around on the page?' The instructor looked up at her. He asked her if she had ever been tested for a learning disability. Maryanne became flustered as it suddenly dawned on her - she had dyslexic tendencies. Here she was a highly successful adult, but when she looked back at her schooling it seemed she had always had to try harder than everybody else in her class. She had thought it was just her. It was an incredible discovery.

How Can I Tell If My Child Has Dyslexia Or If It's Something Else?

Maybe your child is a poor speller. Does that mean they have a learning disability or just a difficulty with spelling? Maybe your child hates to read and dreads reading aloud in class. Does this mean they have dyslexia? Perhaps they just can't seem to grasp numbers concepts and maths problems.

Schoolwork should become challenging for nearly all children at some time or another. If schoolwork never became difficult, it would indicate that teachers are not doing their jobs and providing enough challenges to encourage children to develop their brains.

As parents, we also have the issue of not being sure what to expect from our children. Often the only indicator we have as to how our child is going at school is to compare them to other children, whether they are siblings, family friends or classmates. Unfortunately your child's school reading levels, test and report results are also not a very accurate way of determining whether your child has a learning disability.

"You need to understand that learning disabilities usually affect a range of skills and abilities and there is generally a range of evident symptoms to reflect this. Remember, you need to be concerned about your child if they have an ongoing, significant difficulty with a particular set of basic skills in reading, writing and/or mathematics."

The word 'ongoing' is very subjective. For me as a parent it would mean for 4-6 months. My son could not recognise any of his basic sight words after 4 months and my alarm bells started to ring, prompting me to investigate further. Sight words are basic words often given to young children on flash cards to learn, such as 'the', 'said', and 'my'. They are generally difficult to sound out and make up approximately 25% of all written and spoken language.

What To Look For When You Think Your Child May Be Dyslexic

Please remember a learning disability is never black and white. Your child is an individual, different to you and every other child. They may be displaying some, many or all of the following traits.

Here's what you can look for. Place a marker in the box if you believe your child may exhibit a particular individual trait. This can help you to establish a pattern of behaviour and help you to clarify your thoughts.

Dyslexic Indicators For Pre-Schoolers

- Has difficulty learning and remembering nursery rhymes.
- Can't sit still or listen to stories.
- Likes listening to stories, but never comments on the words or letters.
- Loves listening to stories and can memorise the text of favourite stories without any association to the words.
- Has difficulty learning the alphabet song and mixes up the order of the letters.
- May have difficulty making connections between letters and sounds.
- Cannot recognise the letters in their own name.
- Never comments on word or letters in their environment, such as on TV, computers or in advertising.
- Has no interest in trying to write letters or words.
- Has difficulty drawing or copying basic geometric shapes.
- Is constantly clumsy, lacking coordination and general body awareness.
- Finds it difficult to use scissors, crayons, paintbrushes, etc.
- Has trouble counting or learning to identify written numbers.
- Has a history of slow speech development and has trouble being understood by strangers.
- Has difficulty keeping time or rhythm with sound patterns, such as clapping, music or a regular beat.
- Finds it hard to follow more than one instruction at a time.
- Has difficulty understanding the meaning of words such as underneath, beside, around, above, behind, etc.
- Has trouble locating familiar objects in the home.
- Has difficulty putting items away where they belong.
- Forgets the names of people, places, teachers, colours, and shapes, etc.

DyslexiaDaily.com

- Cannot pronounce sounds to learn new words.
- Puts clothes on the wrong way round.
- Has trouble with gross motor skills such as catching, kicking, throwing, hopping, galloping, skipping, etc.
- When speaking, regularly mixes up familiar words like 'pootfrints' instead of 'footprints'.
- Uses baby talk for longer than would be expected.
- Has an immediate family member who also displays difficulty with reading, writing and spelling.

Please be aware that it is very common for young children up to the age of 6-7 years to write letters, words and whole sentences backwards. That is, from right to left instead of left to right. This is known as 'transposing'. It is perfectly normal for backwards writing and sometimes reading to occur on occasion. If you point it out to your child, they may acknowledge their mistake and giggle. It is important not to reprimand your young child for making this mistake, as you always want to encourage them to 'have a go' when learning to write, whether they make mistakes in their writing or not. All attempts at writing need to be celebrated and this is a normal part of writing and reading development. It is not considered an indicator of dyslexia, unless it occurs very regularly or into their later elementary school years.

Dyslexic Indicators For Elementary Or Primary School Students

- Doesn't enjoy going to school.
- Comes home from school most days exhausted, disagreeable and stressed.
- Gets very stressed and anxious as holidays come to an end and a new school term/year approaches.
- Is extremely tired at the beginning of the school year, terms and semesters.
- Appears to be trying really hard at school, but is not making good progress.

- Has trouble learning and reading basic frequently used sight words such as; my, the, in, on, can, we, to, at, be, etc., often given on flashcard to new school starters.

- Is slow to write their name.

- When reading and writing will often mix up letters in words and may read and write numbers, letters and words backwards. For example 'b' can be seen as 'b', 'd', 'p', 'q' or even '9'.

- When writing or copying written words, has trouble seeing the spaces between the words - they all seem to run together.

- Continues to rely heavily on pictures and illustrations in readers and books.

- Is hesitant and laboured when reading aloud.

- Guesses wildly when reading unknown words instead of trying to sound them out.

- When attempting to sound out unknown words will often confuse the sounds of the letters or letter blends – for example 'sh' for 'ch'.

- Misses whole words when reading aloud. This can be random words or even just the smaller words.

- Mixes up smaller words when reading and may read 'for' instead of 'from' or 'and' instead of 'am'.

- Can learn a word (with parent or teacher help) on a page in their reader and then cannot recognise the same word on the following pages.

- Will regularly read words backwards, such as 'was' for 'saw' or 'no' for 'on'.

- When reading, changes difficult words to a shorter version. For example Katherine becomes Kate.

- May skip parts of words when reading, for example will read 'there' instead of 'thermometer'.

- Continually fails to recognise familiar words.

- Memorises whole stories to avoid processing words and reading.

DyslexiaDaily.com

- Has difficulty knowing the correct beginnings and endings for words. For example they can read 'hop' but not 'hopping'.
- Can be easily distracted and lack concentration in the classroom.
- Cannot focus on a task or a piece of work for a period of time, meaning the work doesn't get completed.
- May have difficulty copying words from the blackboard/whiteboard. Unable to copy long word sequences and copies slowly letter by letter or word part by word part.
- Needs a quiet place with no distractions in order to read or produce any work.
- Has difficulty following a series of instructions.
- Confuses left and right.
- Has a fear of becoming lost.
- Has trouble thinking of words when they are speaking or writing.
- When talking, over uses words such as 'stuff' or 'things', when having difficulty thinking of a word.
- Has a limited vocabulary.
- Produces messy work, with poor handwriting and many crossings out.
- Doesn't hold their pencil correctly.
- Makes poor reading progress compared to the average standard in their class.
- Makes very slow progress with spelling.
- Often spells bizarrely, writing words based on the sounds of the letters and random guesses.
- Has trouble gaining understanding or meaning from written text, also known as reading comprehension.
- Has good comprehension skills when tested verbally, but then cannot write the same answers correctly.
- Isn't able to organise themselves or their possessions.
- Can count aloud, but cannot recognise numbers when written numerically or write them when asked.

- Has difficulty learning their multiplication or times tables.
- Has difficulty learning to tell the time on an analogue clock. They may prefer digital.
- Shows confusion with shape and number patterns, also with number order such as 100's, 10's and 1's.
- Is confused by mathematical symbols such as; + and x and also terms such as; add, subtract, multiply and divide, often mixing them up to produce incorrect answers.
- Has difficulty memorising and remembering things, such as days of the week, months, related seasons, birthdays, names.
- Has difficulty remembering things in sequential order.
- Has poor writing caused by a lack of skill with holding and mastering their pencil or pen.
- Their performance at school is adversely affected by a lack of sleep.
- They have very good or very bad days at school.
- Will try anything to get out of doing their schoolwork.
- Dreads doing homework and gets very stressed and anxious or even angry, requesting your presence and assistance constantly.
- Is easily distracted in order to avoid concentrating on schoolwork.
- May be the class clown, disruptive or withdrawn.
- Enjoys electronic games, but needs constant assistance to play computer or electronic games where the reading of instructions is required.
- May seek constant reassurance by continually asking what is required of them or what is about to happen in terms of future events and schedules.
- Has an immediate family member who also displays difficulty with reading, writing and spelling.

Dyslexic Indicators For Middle, Secondary Or Senior School

Children develop at different rates. For this age group it is also important to consider the indicators listed for primary/elementary school students, as well as the following traits.

- Considers school to be difficult, unsatisfactory and unenjoyable.
- Is excessively tired and disagreeable after school.
- Avoids attending school.
- Is disorganised and forgetful.
- Is hesitant and finds it difficult to read aloud.
- Avoids completing set writing tasks and writes very little.
- Chooses subjects where a minimum of reading, writing and bookwork is required.
- Prefers subjects that allow for mental, physical or hands on creativity.
- May choose shorter more basic words when writing over longer words.
- Their spoken abilities are far superior to their written work.
- Has poor handwriting or writes very slowly.
- Has continued difficulty with spelling.
- Has difficulty with punctuation and grammar.
- Confuses capital and lower case letters when writing.
- Has trouble taking notes or keeping up in class.
- Struggles to organise their study time, complete homework and hand it in on time.
- Lacks strategies to complete set school tasks, organise themselves or to meet deadlines.
- Leaves out words, repeats words or adds in extra words when writing.

- May read slowly or seems to read at quite a good rate, but does not comprehend what they are reading.
- Cannot recognise familiar words.
- Struggles with more complex words like those with prefixes or suffixes.
- When reading, misses lines of text or repeats the same line twice.
- Constantly loses their place when reading and has difficulty locating it again.
- Cannot remember a list of verbal instructions.
- Has trouble with reading, writing and spelling, but displays amazing oral or spoken language skill and may also have an incredible memory.
- May misspell the same word differently in a single piece of writing.
- Is often in the wrong place at the wrong time for no apparent reason.
- Misunderstands complicated instructions or questions.
- Confuses symbols.
- Has trouble with mental maths where time limits are in place.
- May know how to arrive at the correct answer for a complex mathematical equation, but cannot write the steps which led to the final answer.
- Enjoys listening to and playing music, but struggles to read music.
- Has trouble producing work under pressure or where time constraints are in place.
- Can be presented with information in class and then have difficulty deciding what is important.
- Causes trouble at school and displays challenging and difficult behaviour on a regular basis.

- Can often learn foreign languages through listening, mimicking and memorising words and phrases, but will display extreme difficulty when trying to read and write a foreign language.

- Brings home a poor school report card regularly.

- Has an immediate family member who also displays difficulty with reading, writing and spelling.

Why Parents Need To Follow Their Intuition

You may be feeling very confused at this time. You may not know whether your child is exhibiting some of these dyslexic characteristics or to what extent. If this is the case, don't be put off. Make time to do some further investigation.

Talk to your child, ask them questions, do activities with them, spend time listening to them read their readers and library books; make an appointment to speak with your child's teacher. You can ask the teacher for their input and ask to see samples of your child's schoolwork. Make sure you see the proof, your child's actual schoolwork, with your own eyes. It is important for you to understand fully how they are operating at school.

Most teachers will be thrilled to see you taking an active interest in your child and more than happy to work with you in partnership to provide you with answers and help you to assist your child.

If your child's teacher is one of those who seems totally unaware of your child's plight, tries to make excuses, lecture you, or even suggests as a parent you are putting far too much pressure on your child to read and succeed at school, please don't be put off. Be calm, persistent and firm in your request for information. Your child's teacher is a valuable resource and will become an important part of your child's future support system. If, however, you still aren't receiving suitable answers, it's time to go over their head and seek answers from their appropriate superior.

It is always important to listen to your child's teachers and take into consideration what they have to say, but never allow a teacher to intimidate you or to use words you don't understand to answer your questions. This has happened to many parents before you, including me, and it is critical that you are aware of your child's possible learning disability and needs at the earliest possible time. It is highly likely that your child's teacher is not educated enough to recognise all of the dyslexic traits.

Parents generally know their children best and most know, through observing their child and spending time with them, if something is not quite right. Many parents have a strong understanding and even intuition when their child is not operating at their full potential. In many instances parents of children with dyslexia may also have dyslexia or recognise a family history of it and can see similar traits occurring in their own children.

> **"If we don't change our direction we're likely to end up where we're headed."**
>
> Old Chinese Proverb

Author's Story

My eldest son started school at the age of 6. He went into a classroom of 50 students with two teachers, team teaching. After he had been at school for nearly 4 months, he still could not recognise any of the 30 or so basic sight words that were being sent home on flash cards and couldn't read any of the words in his readers. I knew there was a problem so I went to speak to his teachers after school.

I told them what was occurring with my son at home and to be honest they were extremely surprised, because they had no idea. I was then shocked that they had no knowledge of my son's struggle and told them so. Immediately, one of the teachers started to lecture me about the teaching of reading. She did not know I was a trained school teacher. On and on she went, reeling off her knowledge of how children learn to read. She was not making any sense at all, throwing

DyslexiaDaily.com

in words like phonics, syntax, phonemes, semantics and quite honestly none of what she said made any logical sense to me.

I stood there amazed and when she stopped to draw breath, I jumped in, explaining to her that what she had just said to me did not in any way explain to me how to help my child. It may have been my imagination, but I'm sure she looked a little surprised when I explained I was a school teacher and that I felt that my son had problem with learning.

I directed my gaze to the other teacher, who up until this point had remained speechless. He very quickly told me that he understood my concern and would endeavour to monitor my son a little more closely during class time. With that I left, my meeting was over. As I sat in my car, reflecting on what had happened, the worry set in and the tears began to flow.

To this day, I firmly believe that teachers should be able to tell parents when their child is struggling to learn at school within an appropriate time frame.

Although I found this whole situation worrying and frustrating, this experience was the trigger to begin my journey to further educate myself as to how I could help my son. This book is a direct result of that education.

> **"Most of the important things in the world have been accomplished by people who have kept on trying when there seemed to be no hope at all."**
>
> Dale Carnegie

How To Deal With Feelings Of Parental Guilt

Most parents are not qualified teachers, so don't despair if the following describes your situation. There will always be instances where the first time a busy working parent knows there is a problem is via a poor report card, or even a series of poor report cards. Sometimes we can be called in to see the teacher on a number of occasions because of uncharacteristic bad behaviour before we realise something is not quite right. Don't be too hard on yourself. Have faith in yourself and your child. Take that completely normal parental guilt we all suffer from time to time and put it to good use. It doesn't matter how you come to the conclusion something is not quite right with your child's learning ability, what is important is that you do something about it as soon as possible and that is NOW.

If you are not sure if your child has enough of the characteristics to be conclusive, don't worry. This is just the start of beginning to understand and monitor your child. If they are struggling at school, it is time to understand why. Whether it is dyslexia, another learning disability or something completely unrelated, now is the time to act and the process you need to go through is similar, regardless of their troubles.

> **"Every passing minute is another chance to turn your child's life around."**
>
> Liz Dunoon

Chapter 2

My child is showing some
of the dyslexic characteristics.
What do I do now?

Dealing With Our Emotions When We Realise Our Child Might Be Struggling For Legitimate Reasons

This is time of great uncertainty and also confusion. Please understand that many parents have been in this position before you. Regardless of this fact, you may be feeling many different strong emotions; overwhelmed, concerned, guilty, angry, desperate, defensive, protective, upset, and emotional. Maybe you're even feeling a little relieved, that through your own research you might have discovered why your child is not learning as well as others. Now you can work out what to do to help them.

Some of you will feel like you knew that something was not quite right all along and feel relieved because you are finally getting some answers as to what might be wrong with your child.

> **"Some of you will feel like you have just been punched in the stomach, because maybe it's official, your child does have a learning disability. Does this mean they have a life of hardship and no future to look forward to?"**

Others will be feeling just plain confused, because they have no idea what to do next. It is also perfectly understandable and normal if you feel overwhelmed. If your child has been struggling for some time and you have no knowledge of dyslexia and how it may be impacting on your child, it is a worrying time.

Beware Of Well-Meaning People Who Slow You Down

Often as parents we will try to understand and solve our children's difficulties by talking with our family, other parents, friends and even teachers to clarify our own thoughts and to seek their opinions. Although this can be helpful, **BE CAREFUL.** You need to understand that there have been many advances in the study of dyslexia and other learning disabilities in the last 5-10 years. Your child is an individual and it is important not to get caught up in what others may or may not think.

Many common myths exist about dyslexia and many people have their own opinion and definition of what it is. Unfortunately, many of these are incorrect and often too simple to even begin to really describe what it means to be dyslexic. Don't be misled or allow these people to side-track you and slow you down. In order to help your child and get the facts, you need to start your own research and seek the opinion of an expert as soon as possible.

Where Do I Find The Time Or The Money To Deal With Dyslexia?

I'm sure there are those of you who are concerned about the time and money required to deal with this issue. I'm sure there are some of you who have suspected for some time that your child had a learning disability and did not know how to tackle it and so did nothing, or decided to opt for a 'let's wait and see' approach. We are all guilty of making excuses for our children and finding plenty of reasons why they may not be coping at school. This is not a time for guilt, although it is a normal by-product of good parenting; this is a time for action. Please remember that the knowledge you will gain from reading this and other recommended books, as well as the websites and resources provided, will give you the confidence you need to help your child.

> **"The time it takes to turn your child into a happy, confident, changed human being can be as short as a matter of months. Educated, supportive parents are the difference; it is as simple as that."**

Some money and time will be required to get it right, but if you spend your money carefully and use your time wisely, it will be an investment that will pay enormous dividends. That is what this book is for, to give you the confidence to help you to understand where to start, what you should spend your money on and what to do next. It is the beginning of your education and through this, your child's enormous, everyday struggle with their education might just slowly begin to subside.

Remember though, there is no miracle overnight cure. Not yet anyway. Many children with dyslexia feel like they are constantly hitting their heads against a brick wall as they try to cope with school tasks. Some of them have even stopped looking at the walls, because it becomes too stressful and too difficult to even consider overcoming such huge learning obstacles. By becoming educated, you are giving your child an incredible gift. You will help them to begin to see over the tops of those walls and perhaps even lower them so they can get right over.

"Having you on their team is really what matters to your struggling child. It will make them feel more confident and more capable to tackle those walls that they face every day and we all know,

CONFIDENCE IS KING."

How Can I Possibly Learn All I Need To Know About Dyslexia To Support My Child?

When you begin this journey of dyslexic discovery, you may lack confidence and feel like it is such a huge responsibility that you can't possibly achieve it. Maybe you're thinking you do not have the education, the emotional strength or the time it takes to really help your child. And what happens if you get it wrong?

Don't let excuses hold you back. If it helps, look at it like this. When we are at secondary school, college or university, we complete a series of subjects each year. Some we choose, they are called electives, such as Drama and Woodwork, and other subjects are compulsory, like Mathematics and English. You have just chosen to study an elective subject, your child and dyslexia; just one subject, for the whole year.

DyslexiaDaily.com

The time and effort required to study this can be likened to going back to school to study just one subject. You will read (or listen to) about the same number of books, make notes, research and spend time talking to teachers and specialists. The best part is you get to decide how to gauge your success in this subject. It may be your child's newfound happiness and increasing confidence levels, or a particular success in a certain subject area.

> **"Don't allow helping and supporting your child to become a task so frightening that you do not feel you can do it; remember to keep it in perspective. Once you start this journey you will find hundreds of other parents who are doing exactly the same thing - helping their children with dyslexia to be successful."**

So here's what you need to do to get started.

How To Create A Diary And A Research File For Your Child With Dyslexia

This does not have to take months to put together, although it should be an ongoing collection of information. It doesn't need to be too time consuming either. Your daily diary, some plastic pocket folders, a plastic storage tub and a note or exercise book is about all you will need. Get started with those items you already have.

- **Take notes** - Use the diary or notepad that you use on a daily basis to jot down and date quick notes to describe a difficulty your child may be having with a task. These notes will become a valuable resource to help identify what your child's weaknesses are and will help to determine what support and assistance they may require.

- **Keep track of school reports** - Put any past assessments or school reports into one date ordered plastic pocket folder.

- **Start collecting examples of your child's work -** This can include schoolwork, project work, artwork, computer work even photos of items they have created. This collection is important. Make sure it is dated and labelled. Through it you will begin to see patterns of your child's learning and understanding. Ask teachers to make sure they send home your child's work from time to time so you can see it, or drop by the classroom and collect it for yourself. Often children work in workbooks which need to remain at school for the whole year. When they finally do arrive home, go through them and photocopy or cut pages out for your file. Collect pages which show what they do well and what they struggle with. Make a list to help you summarise their school strengths and weaknesses.

- **Talk to your child -** Sit down with your child and ask them what they find hard and what they find easy. Your child is smart and they generally know which tasks they love at school and which they hate. You can use the list of dyslexic indicators as a prompt to give you an idea of any questions you may like to ask your child. Make a list of these. If they are too little to do this yet, watch, listen and observe them at play, at home and at school.

- **Talk to teachers -** Make a time to speak to all your child's classroom teachers, including specialist teachers. Ask them to tell you what your child's strengths and weaknesses are. School reports are helpful to a point, but you need detail. Ask them to use the school curriculum. The curriculum is a school document that describes what your child will be taught in each subject during a particular year level. Ask teachers to give you specifics. By doing this you may begin to feel empowered. This process will give you a good and positive feeling and it is a great place for you to start. It also lets the teachers know you are seeking answers from them regarding your child's learning difficulties and ensures they understand that they need to be accountable. This can assist you in future by making your child's teachers more conscientious and thoughtful regarding your child. You need to develop a positive and open line of communication with your child's teachers, as this is important for your future success in helping your child. You may need to consider giving the teachers some forewarning of what you are seeking, via a note, email or phone, before you arrive. This will give them time to prepare some information for you. This way you will get a better, more considered response from them.

- **Make a detailed list of all your child's strengths** - This list is very important and will be even better if you can give examples of how your child demonstrates these strengths. Make it a list that you add to constantly. Make sure it includes everything; consider academic strengths, social strengths, personality strengths, sporting or physical strengths and family strengths. Nothing should be missed. Start watching them and adding to the list when you see they are doing something really well. Don't forget to ask other valued people what they consider your child's strengths to be. The close family dynamic between a child and a parent or carer can often change the way children behave and conduct themselves in your presence. Ask others outside of your immediate family, whose opinion you trust and value, to contribute to your list. You might just be pleasantly surprised by what you hear. No strength is too small or irrelevant to be included. This important list can become the basis for any future decisions you may make regarding your child's education and future. It may even show you what you need to do next to help them learn, increase their confidence and to begin to experience more success.

- **Make a detailed list of all your child's weaknesses** - It is also important to make a list of your child's weaknesses. Make this more in point form and, if you can, include an example of how this weakness was demonstrated or identified. This will help you later to put strategies in to place to help your child compensate for and overcome these weaknesses. You will also see that a weakness like a reluctance to write can be easily overcome if one of your child's strengths is excellent word processing skills. It may not be that your child has nothing to say, more that writing it with a pen or pencil is too difficult for them. Another example is a child who is terrible at their times tables when writing down the answers, but has a high accuracy rate if they are allowed to answer verbally.

- **Create a collection of resources that supports your child's strengths -** Put together a collection of items that support your child's strengths. You can include such things as certificates, medals, ribbons, awards, audio files of singing or music, videos of their performances, blueprints of designs they have created, letters of recommendation, references, trophies and so on. Sometimes the best place for this collection is where your child can see it, on a bedroom wall or on a shelf. This will then serve as a constant reminder of all the things they do well.

This research file is critical. It can show you so much about your child that you need to see and to focus on. You can make your child aware of the research file if you choose and ask them to help you to include items that they are satisfied, happy with and proud of.

> **"Sometimes as parents we get so caught up in the fact that our child is struggling at school that we stop being balanced in our view of them as people."**

A learning disability can be overwhelming for families, parents and children. Sometimes, focusing on our children's strengths can put their weaknesses back into perspective. Strengths are also a great focus to have when we want to help our children to be successful.

Chapter 3

How to get an accurate diagnosis for your struggling child.

The Importance Of Getting An Accurate Diagnosis

The one endorsement in this book to spend any money is right here. You must have your child's learning disability diagnosed accurately; it is as simple as that. Accurate, age appropriate testing can be conducted from as early as 6 or 7 years of age and, according to The International Dyslexia Association, even earlier.

Don't be put off testing early. The decision to do so may wipe out years of being misunderstood and struggling to learn. Dyslexia is complex and can range from extremely severe to relatively mild. You need to know the exact nature of your child's condition in order to help them. Just because a parent or grandparent has dyslexia or has learning difficulties does not mean your child with dyslexia will be affected in the same way. Never assume family members will be the same. In a world full of different learning challenges, you need to know exactly what is influencing your child's ability to learn or to struggle with learning. Your child's strengths will also be uncovered in more detail, which is often the key to helping your child succeed.

Every state of every English speaking country in the world has a different set of legal standards for dyslexic students. It pays to be aware of your legal rights. Dyslexia assessments are a legal right for a child with 'special education needs' in the UK and children with 'specific learning disabilities' in the USA. In the UK and USA, parental involvement in the assessment process is also ensured by legislation.

In the UK, the 1981 Education Act allows parents to request a free assessment for their child if they have a 'special educational need' - that is significantly greater difficulty in learning than the majority of children their age.

In the USA, a free evaluation prior to the creation of an educational plan is one of the key provisions of Public Law 94-142.

If you are considering a private school, it is worthwhile discussing the school's individual policy and level of support for students with dyslexia.

In other states and countries the law isn't so definitive. Dyslexia assessments can still be obtained, but this is not a legal right.

Why Parents Must Be The Driving Force

Remember though, it is never too late to have an older child or adult assessed. The tests used provide an incredible amount of useful information. They can be life changing.

> **"There is no doubt about it - the fastest way to get your child tested is to pay for it and get a private assessment. If you have the money, I would strongly recommend that you do this and the sooner the better. The earlier the assessment the better the outcome for your child will be."**

In a perfect world where money is no object, I am sure that we would all act quickly and go private. Why is it so hard to get my child tested, I hear you ask? Why does it take so long and have to be so expensive? These are very good questions. Wouldn't it be wonderful to have a magic wand to make getting tested for dyslexia and other learning disabilities easily accessible and free for everyone? Imagine a day when this type of testing can be conducted in a child's first year of school for free as part of the learning program. Then as parents we could begin to assist and support our child from day one and teachers could teach to suit our child's learning style.

Unfortunately this is not the case, well, not yet anyway. The fact is that parents often have to prove that their child is struggling and has fallen a long way behind their classmates before they can get a free assessment provided by the government. To add to this, the waiting times can be long and frustrating. The same can apply for teachers who know that a student is struggling and, with or without the parent's consent, is seeking a diagnosis on their student's behalf.

It is important to realise however, that as a parent or guardian you must often be the driver when it comes to seeking help for your struggling child. This is not to say that there aren't some excellent caring teachers in our schools. There are many, however there are also many students to teach and many demands are made on a dedicated teacher's time in the current education system. So it often comes back to the parents to represent their children and seek action on their behalf.

Why You Need To Know If Your Child Has A Learning Disability Or Not

It seems to be a general worldwide trend that there is a reluctance to label children with a specific learning disability and most parents will have their own view on this. The outcome of this reluctance to label is this: without some form of diagnosis and recognised label, your child may never receive the level of assistance they are entitled to from the relevant education authority. Regardless of the extent of their dyslexia or learning disability, wouldn't you want them to receive as much assistance as is available to them while they are at school?

> **"Childhood, youth and formal education is such a short phase of a person's long life. However we all know that what happens during these years can determine the adult they will become, the attitudes, skills and confidence they will develop and the future they can look forward to."**

Ultimately it is a parent's choice whether their child will be tested or not and whether you want a label to be applied or not. Just don't waste the opportunity to help your child as early as you can. It is the one time when being a pushy parent can be a major positive and it can be critical when it means the difference between your child being given extra assistance or not.

Even if you don't have a definite diagnosis or label, or you have to wait to see a specialist, your child can receive extra assistance from teachers, educational specialists and parents if they are struggling to learn and are not reaching educational benchmarks. There is also no reason why you can't begin to offer your child some assistance at home.

Please remember that many experts define dyslexia as a complex brain-processing problem which needs to be diagnosed accurately by specialists with the appropriate qualifications. When your child is at school in their classroom, most teachers see only their behaviour and the schoolwork they produce. This can illustrate the symptoms of certain brain processing problems, but it is not and never will be an accurate way to diagnose dyslexia.

Who Is Qualified To Test Your Child For Dyslexia?

- An in-school learning support teacher or counsellor with the appropriate postgraduate qualifications. You need to check qualifications thoroughly. If you require further clarification, check with the dyslexic association in your state or territory.

- A developmental paediatrician, although you may need a referral from your family doctor.

- A developmental child psychologist.

- An educational neuropsychologist.

- An educational psychologist, who may be allocated to assist you through your Government Education Department.

- A children's hospital will often have a department specifically for children with development or specific learning disabilities, where all the appropriate specialists are available. This could include paediatricians, psychologists, social workers, speech therapists, physiotherapists, nurses, teachers and others. These departments often have close links with education authorities. This means you may not need further testing and will receive a comprehensive report covering all aspects of your child's learning disability, support services and what you can do to support them effectively.

- A private clinic that specialises in the diagnosis of children's developmental and learning disabilities, specifically dyslexia.

How To Choose The Right Dyslexia Assessor

Now this is important. Just because a person is qualified to test for a specific learning disability such as dyslexia, it does not automatically make them the best person to assess your particular child. If you have the ability to choose, the importance of finding the right person can be critical for your child, so you need to conduct some research. Not only do they need to have the right qualifications so you get exactly what you need in the way of an accurate diagnosis, they must also have the right personality to suit you and your child.

If you just don't have this option and are referred to a specialist within your education system, you can still be well informed as to what form the assessment will take, who will conduct it and what you will get out of it.

The individual or team who assesses your child must have a proven track record in assessing and diagnosing learning disabilities. They must have a knowledge and background in psychology, reading, language and education. They must be aware of the latest research, educational and medical advances in the area of dyslexia. They must also have knowledge of how individuals learn to read and an understanding of what it is that causes people to struggle to learn. They must know how to measure learning and language difficulties and your child's general intelligence, in order to make an accurate diagnosis and recommendation.

Conducting Research To Locate A Good Dyslexia Assessor

You can get started by speaking to others about what you are seeking. Talk to other parents, teachers, learning support teachers, school principals, family members and friends. You can even get in contact with other schools if yours is not being helpful. Learning difficulties are so common that it is not hard to find people who can point you in the right direction.

"In this field of work it is possible to find the most incredible and dedicated professionals with an intricate knowledge of a range of learning disabilities and an amazing understanding of how it feels to be dyslexic. These individuals are often not in the job of assessing and diagnosing learning disabilities for the money, but for the rewarding opportunity to change people's lives for the better."

These people do exist and if you can find an individual like this, you and your child are indeed blessed.

Next, you need to understand and decide what it is you want to get out of your child's assessment. Money and time are also a big issue for most parents, so if you have the resources to go private, you need to be sure that any money you spend or time that you take off work gives you exactly what you are seeking.

Remember you can shop around. You are a customer and you want the best professional and the best result for the time money and effort you are putting in. Prices will vary and so will the personality of the specialist, the time they allocate to you, their effort and the test results you receive.

So how do you shop around? Where do you look? You can jump on the internet. Type *dyslexia testing* into the search engine, as well as the area or state in which you live. See what comes up and then make some phone calls, speak to people and get them to send you some information. You may also be able to access contact details through your local school, or ring or email your local Education Department office for a list of recommended specialists. Check the telephone directory and don't forget to check out this book's resource directory at www.dyslexiadaily. com. There is a good chance you will find what you are seeking there.

The Dyslexia Assessment

Having a formal diagnosis of your child's learning disability is a must if you want to ensure your child has access to all the educational considerations that are available to them. As parents, this is an important part of ensuring your child is provided with the best possible opportunity to succeed within the school system. Beware of people working within the school system who deter you from seeking a formal diagnosis. They are often not qualified to do so and if your child does not have a formal diagnosis, then it just so happens that your child's learning disability does not have to be catered for in its entirety by the school your child attends. You can liken the assessment to having a legal document which states the exact nature of your child's condition and their rights. Now you might be beginning to understand why only highly qualified individuals with legitimate qualifications are able to assess children for dyslexia. The range of tests used must also be recognised and endorsed by the Education Department within your state. All these factors invariably add up financially, meaning the cost of having your child assessed is higher than you might expect.

A formal diagnostic assessment report is based on a battery of tests. Depending on the assessor, these could be administered over the course of one day or over a series of days. Different assessors use a range of different tests, but your evaluation should include:

- A case history that includes information on family history, development, medical history, behaviour and academic background
- A measure of intellectual functioning – also known as an intelligence test
- Tests of specific oral language skills related to reading, writing ability and a phonological test
- Educational tests to determine levels of functioning and ability in the basic skill areas of reading, spelling, written language and math. Testing in reading and writing should include the following measures:
- Single word decoding of real and nonsense words
- Oral and silent reading in context

- Reading comprehension
- Spelling in isolation and in text
- Sentence, story and essay writing
- Handwriting
- A classroom observation, and a review of any remediation programs used to date
- Many assessors will also recognise the need to explore the potential of visual dyslexia - that is where distortions of text and text movement can be occurring

How Do I Explain The Dyslexic Assessment To My Child?

Children who struggle at school often find the idea of assessments uncomfortable. They may feel that these tests are going to prove once and for all that they are completely stupid and everyone is going to know about it. You need to allay these fears. It's all about the way you explain what is going to happen. Here are some ideas to help you:

- 'There are no right or wrong answers to these tests – you can't fail'
- 'The results of the tests are confidential, the children at school don't even need to know about them'
- 'These tests are specially designed - they will give us some answers as to why you find some tasks at school so difficult'
- 'These tests will help us to clarify how you like to learn'
- 'These tests will help your teachers at school to understand how best to teach you and what style of activities you prefer when learning'
- 'These tests will tell us your strengths as well as your weaknesses so we will know what we need to do to help you through school'
- 'Often children who struggle at school do so for very real reasons. Sometimes it's because they learn differently – if the tests show that this is the case for you, the school will give you more help'

- 'We know you are clever even though you struggle at school. These tests will tell us how clever you are for your age'
- 'The person who will be assessing you is independent of the school system. It is their job to make your life easier, not more difficult'
- 'It won't be all reading and writing; you will get to do lots of different activities'
- 'Let's face it, it's a day off school and I will take you and bring you home'

Who Should Attend The Meeting After The Dyslexia Assessment To Receive The Results?

It is a must for all active parents and carers of the child who is experiencing learning difficulties to attend the appointment where the results are given and strategies to assist are discussed. That could be mum and/or dad, a close family friend, a grandparent, extended family or direct carers such as foster parents.

This cannot be stressed enough. Often this task is left to just one parent or family member, as not everyone else sees the need to take time off work and be present. There is no doubt that the more active parents or carers that have this first-hand information, the more effective your team-like assistance to your child will be.

I implore you to invest one day in the life of your child to ensure you are all on the same support team from day one. This is not something you should compromise on. Another parent or carer, through a sheer lack of knowledge and understanding, can undo all the hard work of an educated parent very easily and unwittingly. Don't allow this to happen to your child.

What You Should Receive After Your Child's Dyslexia Assessment

It doesn't matter whether the assessment is done through the Education Department or privately; you need to ensure you receive the following:

- A thorough understanding of your child's learning strengths and weaknesses in plain simple language that you can understand. You need to receive a copy of the actual report, as well as a clear verbal explanation of the results, to ensure your understanding. Make sure you read Chapter 4, 5, 13 & 14 of this book before you go, so that you will understand dyslexia in all its forms. This will ensure you ask all the right questions of the specialists and understand the complicated jargon.

- An assessment result of your child's general level of intelligence.

- A detailed set of test results and related documents which will define your child's processing difficulties in intricate detail.

- The same test results should determine your child's ability to access special education services available in schools in your particular state or territory. These results and the diagnosis can also determine your child's ongoing eligibility for special considerations and programs in secondary schools, colleges and universities.

- A suggested list of teaching methods that can be applied to your child in school and at home.

- Any referrals to specialists that your child may require.

- A detailed list of resources including books, websites and teaching aids which may benefit your child.

Watch Out For Information Overload

A note of warning here, you only need to be made aware of those resources that can help your child specifically. There are literally thousands of resources available for children with learning disabilities. I'm sure many of you have already been on the internet and have come away overwhelmed and confused by all that is available.

At the meeting after your assessment to receive your child's results it can become a confusing and extremely expensive minefield and you may be making buying decisions based on emotion rather than clear thinking.

Beware Of Sales People

Unfortunately, there are some people who seek to make large amounts of money from your fragile emotional state and your child's learning disability. Consider carefully what your child can cope with or really needs. Children with dyslexia are often mentally exhausted after a day at school. When you are considering the purchase of a resource or learning program, make sure you see a direct connection between what is being offered and how it will help your child specifically. If you can't see a connection I recommend that you don't part with your hard-earned cash.

There are only so many hours in the day that your child can learn. Do not spend any extra money unless you can see a suitable product with a direct benefit for your child, which suits their personality and learning style. Throwing lots of money at specialists or buying expensive learning resources as a way of helping your dyslexic child is not going to make the dyslexia go away, or ease your high levels of anxiety and emotion. At this time your child needs an ongoing commitment from you, not your money.

> **"If you choose to buy any learning or teaching resources, they must be directly beneficial, time efficient, fun and rewarding, or all three."**

Teaching resources must provide your child with instant results and teach them in a way that suits them and your family's lifestyle. I recommend that before you make any purchasing decisions, you take a few days to read your child's report, think about it and talk to family members, teachers and any other specialist on your support team. You can always purchase learning resources at a later date after you have processed the report and all the details and decided how best to help your child. Many resources are also available for free if you know where to look.

How To Create A Simple Action Plan To Help Your Child

'Simple' is the key word when creating this plan. If it's too complicated, takes too much planning or time to put into action, there is a good chance it won't happen at all. Maybe you will start full of good intentions and then your job, housework, ballet practise, soccer training or just plain exhaustion will get in the way. It really does have to be simple. So what are the features of a simple plan that you need to consider?

"Regular practise not only makes perfect. It also makes learning permanent."

Aim to allow for ten minutes of time each day. Create short, sharp blocks of ten minute activities you can do with your son or daughter. It can be one ten minute session per day or two or three depending on your child and your available time. I recommend short sessions each day simply because it's more easily achievable. It is important to understand that it should never become a drag for either party.

Ten minutes can be utilised in bed before your child sleeps at night, before school, after school, while you are waiting at the train station or in the car to pick up another child from music practise. It's do-able for busy parents and tired children.

"Daily repetitive practise to learn and remember new information has a simple, scientifically proven premise – brain neurons that fire together wire together, helping to make learning permanent."

- Plan when you will do it – if you write it down, it is more likely to happen. Don't make too much of a fuss about it. Put the emphasis on spending time together with your son or daughter, not working on tasks to overcome dyslexia – this should be the outcome.

- Consider others who can assist you in providing a session each day if you have restrictions on your time. Make it someone your child likes or looks up to. It could be your spouse, partner, supportive siblings, extended family, the mature teenager up the street who is looking for some extra cash, paid or unpaid tutors or teachers or teacher aides who can help before or after school. Childcare workers can also be a great resource, as can past teachers and family friends. Many activities can also be utilised, which do not require constant supervision. You can get them started and then make a note of their results at the end.

- Now consider your child's dyslexic strengths and weakness. If you have your diagnostic report, refer to it. If not, use your knowledge of what you child does well to provide you with the key to what type of activities will be effective and how you need to teach them.

- To decide what skills you are going to cover, you could take direction from your child, your child's teacher or you could utilise your own observations. You can focus on one skill like spelling, or choose a range across subject and skill areas. In Chapter 17 we discuss how to identify your child's main issue of concern – sometimes this is a good place to start.

- You also have to consider whether you are going to teach your child based on their current school work, for instance spelling words or times tables for that week, or will your emphasis be on teaching them skills for long term education? Are you more concerned with a higher mark for their spelling test at school that week or teaching spelling skills for life? There is no right or wrong answer here. Maybe you could do a bit of both.

- Another important factor to consider is your child's enjoyment level. Your child has enough stress every day just getting through school; there is no need to add to this burden. Research shows that if a child enjoys learning and feels confident and successful during the process, a happy chemical called dopamine is released in their brain. This in turn assists the learning by helping to cement it in their long-term memory.

- Here's why you need to be creative. Schools predominantly teach using static, formal methods. Your child sits still on the mat or at their desk, listens to the instructions and completes the task in their book as described by the teacher. I'm sure you remember this method when you were at school. It does not tend to benefit a dyslexic child, who generally possesses auditory and/or visual processing difficulties. Think outside the square. Teach spelling while your son jumps on a trampoline, use highlighters to circle words in magazines, give your child a whistle to blow every time she sees a full stop when you are reading her a story, use audio books and board games.

For 100's of ideas on how you can quickly and effectively teach your dyslexic child, go to www.dyslexiadaily.com and access the world's biggest internet resource directory available for dyslexics. You will also find free downloadable eBooks on how to reach your dyslexic child to 'Read', 'Write and Spell' and do 'Math'.

- As you develop your action plan (see chapter 19) for your child, consider your goals. If it helps write them down, something like;

'By the end of 3rd term Jack will be typing at 30 words per minute with no errors'.

Or:

'By the 3rd of October, Jill will be able to accurately write and spell 20 of her most used sight words.'

Or it may even be something like:

'By the end of 2nd term, Zach will be happy to go to school.'

- Older children can help you to set these goals, making them more proactive in attempting to meet the target. Alternatively, if goals are not being met it is always important to have a discussion as to why this is the case and how this can be rectified.

- It is a good idea to learn as you go. Be flexible and improve your system as you discover what works for both you and your child.

"In Australia there is no legal right to assessment, but once a child is assessed and diagnosed with dyslexia, then the Anti-Discrimination Act protects children's rights through the Disability Standards for Education 2005. All educational institutions in Australia must provide appropriate support for students diagnosed with a disability including dyslexia."

Margaret Hardy, Dyslexia Testing Services Australia

A Tiny Spark

A tiny spark
A flicker of recognition
A hint of a smile
You know it made sense
You know you got through
A rainbow is forming

by Liz Dunoon

DyslexiaDaily.com

Chapter 4

So what is dyslexia and how do you get it?

Author's Note

Of all the chapters in this book, the next two were the most challenging to write. Why? I hear you ask. The word 'dyslexia' is only one word, but it describes a very complex condition that has been mystifying humankind for over a century. Its existence is recognised by a majority of people worldwide; however there are still those that would prefer to say that it doesn't exist.

Everyone seems to have a differing view, a definition or an experience they relate to when describing or explaining dyslexia. This broad spectrum of understanding makes researching the topic of dyslexia extremely difficult, especially for parents of dyslexic children who are trying to become educated and support a dyslexic child.

Everyone, it seems, offers a different view or a different opinion and tends to support a different course of action, with a range of price tags attached. Perhaps this is why it is so difficult to find a consistent level of understanding and support for your child during their school years.

When you look at a child with dyslexia, you can't tell that they have a learning disability in the way you can with a child who has a physical disability. The symptoms of being dyslexic only become outwardly evident when a child is learning, remembering or demonstrating a cognitive or physical skill. The confusion is compounded because no two dyslexic people will ever exhibit the exact same set of symptoms.

Even the experts disagree on how prevalent dyslexia is, how to define it, test for it, teach people with it and whether it can be cured or not.

So where does that leave parents who are trying to understand dyslexia so they can help their children? Well, like you, I have dyslexic children to support. Being a teacher who is fascinated by the process of learning and language acquisition, I started researching until I found some consistent, accessible answers which would enable me to help my children. I realised very quickly that the best place to start was with my children and their unique set of dyslexic traits. My aim was to make them happy to go to school, successful and positive about the future.

Why Are So Many Books About Dyslexia Outdated?

I started reading books on the topic of dyslexia and how the brain operates. Fortunately, I love to read, because many of the books were so complicated my head hurt. Then I started to speak to teachers, specialist educators and dyslexia assessors. Throughout this process, I was constantly using the internet to see what world recognised dyslexia experts were researching and studying and what the outcomes of those studies were. To be honest with you, it was an amazing and enlightening journey. The more I learnt, the more I needed to know. I quickly came to the conclusion that many of the books in my teaching and dyslexia library were outdated and I am talking books that had only been published in the last 10 years. How could that be? I hear you ask. Well! The answer is relatively simple:

- Learning disabilities like dyslexia are having a major impact on the education system and the success rate of children in our schools.

- Concerned parents are constantly asking questions and seeking answers as to why their child is struggling to learn and what can be done to allow for their child's learning differences.

- Diagnostic testing has become more readily available.

- School teachers and their training and skill levels are being brought into question as it becomes obvious that outdated academic and formal education styles do not suit a large proportion of children.

- Pressure is being applied to Education Departments and governments to provide funding for research into learning disabilities like dyslexia and for on-going teacher training.

- There has been a huge scientific step forward in understanding the human brain and how it works, through the use of functional brain imaging and brain mapping. For the first time, specialists can see how a dyslexic brain is functioning compared to a non-dyslexic brain. This is beginning to impact upon dyslexic research because the effectiveness of learning programs can be properly evaluated.

- A cavernous divide exists between what science currently knows about dyslexia and the methods being used to teach dyslexics in a majority of schools. People are becoming more aware of this and are realising it is time for educational change.

- Many famous people who are publicly recognised as being highly successful have come forward to say they are dyslexic. These people are making a valuable contribution to society yet,by most accounts, were dissatisfied with their schooling, did not do well or left early.

- The age of information technology and the internet is upon us, making information more readily available and allowing us to share our knowledge and understanding.

As my research continued, I identified many exceptional individuals in the fields of science, medicine, psychology and education who are making an incredible contribution to our understanding of what dyslexia is, how it impacts upon people and ways people can overcome it. I say 'overcome it', because there is now evidence to suggest that a person's brain is plastic. Not made of plastic, but a term used to describe the brain's ability to re-organise itself with practise and repetition of tasks to compensate for weaknesses, damage and aging. Known as 'neuroplasticity', this is great news for dyslexics. I will discuss more about this topic in the following chapter.

Much of my understanding of the symptoms of dyslexia has come from my research, teaching children and living in a household of dyslexics, but I don't consider myself to be an expert on the science of dyslexia. To understand the latest specialised knowledge on dyslexia I have consulted the experts.

Who Is John Stein And How Can His Work Help My Struggling Child?

Professor John Stein FRCP, a Professor of neuroscience at Magdalen College, Oxford University, England, is a world renowned leading expert in the study of dyslexia. He has conducted 25 years of research in collaboration with many other specialists, producing hundreds of report papers with the intention of creating a greater understanding of dyslexia and easing the burden of individuals worldwide whose lives are affected by it.

Who Is Silvia Paracchini And How Can Her Work Help My Struggling Child?

Dr. Silvia Paracchini currently works in a research group led by Professor Tony Monaco at the Wellcome Trust Centre For Human Genetics, also located at Oxford University in England. Tony Monaco's group has been studying the genetics of neuro-developmental disorders for many years. Silvia Paracchini is particularly interested in understanding the molecular mechanisms leading to dyslexia and the role genetics play in the prevalence of dyslexia. This relates to how dyslexia can be passed from generation to generation within the same family. Silvia often works closely with John Stein to conduct research studies.

Both of these specialists have generously offered me their expertise and knowledge, to ensure you will have the most up to date knowledge of dyslexia based on their current research and understanding. It is important though to recognise all the collaborators who have been responsible for this work, so please find a list of individuals in the front of this book.

Parents need to have access to recent research in order to know how to offer their children the highest level of support. Remember, it is often the parent who needs to keep their child's classroom teachers up to date too.

It is important to understand that there are various theories on what causes dyslexia and why it exists. Specialists all around the world are continually carrying out new research studies as funding becomes available. As a parent of a child with dyslexia, some theories may make more sense than others when considering your child.

**To stay up to date, check out
www.dyslexiadaily.com for news articles and
research reports. We will continually update this list
as new resources become available.**

A Brief History Of Dyslexia

The word 'dyslexia', comes from the Greek language and basically means 'difficulty with words'. It is thought that the term 'dyslexia' was originally used by a German ophthalmologist in 1887 to describe a specific loss of the ability to read, referred to as 'word blindness'. Word blindness is generally accredited as being discovered by Kussmaul, a German physician, in 1877.

In the United Kingdom in 1896, Pringle-Morgan, a local general medical practitioner, documented the case of a 14 year old boy named Percy. He was described as one of the brightest boys in his class, with exceptional talents in mathematics and oral responses. However he had severe difficulty with reading, writing and spelling. In his report, Pringle-Morgan documents some of Percy's spelling errors as writing 'Precy' for 'Percy', 'seashore' as 'seasons' and 'song' as 'scone'.

Over several subsequent decades, James Hinshelwood, an eye surgeon from Glasgow, continued to promote the idea of 'congenital word blindness', congenital meaning that the trait existed from birth. In his work in 1900, he commented on the high occurrence of the condition, its low rate of recognition and the subsequent harsh treatment of such pupils as 'imbeciles' or 'incorrigibles'. In 1917, he made note of the genetic nature of 'word blindness' and also noted the fact that it occurred more in boys.

In the USA in 1937, Samuel Orton, a neurologist disagreed with the 'word blindness' concept. He is quoted as saying, "…..there is no true blindness in the ordinary sense of the term, nor indeed is there ever blindness for words."

Orton preferred the term 'strephosymbolia', which literally means the twisting of symbols. He began to document reading and spelling transpositions, such as letter reversals and word reversals like 'was' for 'saw', as well as spoonerisms such as 'button cuffs' for 'cuff buttons'.

Samuel Orton, together with Anna Gillingham, pioneered a systematic multisensory teaching program. This concept was further developed in the mid 1970's in Britain by Kathleen Hickey and Beve Hornsby, amongst others, forming the basis of many of the dyslexic teaching programs available to dyslexic students today.

Why Does Dyslexia Exist?

To try to understand why dyslexia exists, we need to look further back into the history of mankind; John Stein tells us that reading and spelling require a phenomenal amount of brainpower. Simply decoding this sentence from symbols to sounds and then into words with meaning, is one of the most complex tasks your brain encounters. The reason for this is that reading is a relatively new invention. "It was invented around 5000 years ago and was piggybacked onto our spoken ability, which was invented 30,000-40,000 years ago. It has only been in the last 200 years that reading has been considered a skill that all individuals were expected to acquire", John Stein says. "This indicates our brains have had to evolve relatively quickly, making new neurological connections and as a result developmental glitches may have occurred in our brains, one of these being dyslexia".

Speaking, it seems, is innate. We as humans have been speaking for tens of thousands of years. All that is necessary to learn to speak is inbuilt from birth. Simply by exposing a baby to spoken language a young child will learn to speak.

Reading on the other hand, is not innate. It is not built into our existing genetic matter; rather it is an invention of humankind and must be learned with skill and effort. Because speech came first and is made up of a large number of spoken sounds, these have been converted into a range of single and blended letters symbols. For example, look at the word 'break'. To read it, we pull apart the sounds based on the letters in the words b--rrr--aaa--k. This conversion of letters to sounds is not an exact science, and with so many influences on the English language as it has evolved, there are huge spelling inconsistencies, making it a difficult language to learn.

Think of words like 'enough', 'champagne', 'psychology', 'said', 'won' and 'one' or 'latte'.

To read, we need to decode the letter symbols back in to their appropriate spoken sounds to gain meaning. It is this link between letter combinations and sounds that seems to prove difficult for dyslexics.

To learn to read, a child must first learn that spoken words can be pulled apart into individual sounds. For example 'dog' is 'duh – ohh – guh'. For approximately 2/3 of children, this knowledge develops without delay by the age of approximately 6-7 years. In contrast, approximately another 1/3 experience difficulty noticing the basic sounds that make up spoken and written words when reading, with many continuing to do so.

When we speak without thinking, we automatically go to our internal dictionary to get the range of sounds required to make a word. We then put them in the correct order and utter the word. For most people this is done automatically and the sounds are crisp and easily understood. Dyslexics attempting to retrieve sound parts for words can experience more of a delay and sometimes the sound parts may seem fuzzy - think of 'f' and 'th'. This can cause errors when speaking and confusion of words.

A child's ability to learn to read is often a determining factor in whether a child is perceived as dyslexic or not. John Stein considers reading to be an extremely difficult skill to acquire. It requires visual identification of letter symbols and their order, rapid decoding into the sounds the letters represent and background knowledge of how words can be broken down into units of sound, yet processed as a complete entity.

For example, to learn to read, write and spell a word such as 'disillusioned', you must be able to break it down like this;

dis-il-lu-sion-ed

Which technically should really look like this;

dis- il-loo-shond

I chose this word because it was in my 9 year old son's school reader. He has visual dyslexia, and this word is a good example of how hard it can be for dyslexics to process and learn new words. My son had no idea how to decode or read this difficult word, yet he must learn to, as he will come across this and similar words time and time again as his reading development continues.

John Stein describes two pathways for reading.

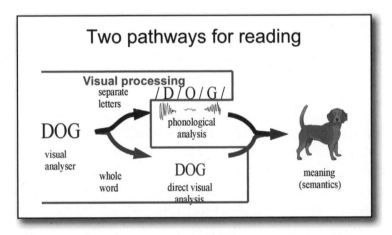

Image Courtesy of Prof. John Stein, Dyslexia Research Trust

A child learning to read invariably breaks down each word into letters such as 'd-o-g', or letter blends like 'th' or 'sh'. They then sound the word out, putting all the individual sounds together to make the word meaningful. This is known as the phonics approach to reading because it relies on knowing the sounds of the letters in the words. Words which cannot be sounded out, such as 'the' and 'said' are invariably learnt using memorisation techniques like 'rote learning'. These methods require a large amount of practise, concentration and mental energy.

A practised, experienced reader does not have to sound out familiar words like 'dog' using the phonics approach. Once they have been exposed to the word on a certain number of occasions, it becomes stored in their long term memory, never again requiring to be broken down and sounded out. It can be automatically recalled, making reading fluent and effortless.

Dyslexics have to learn to read while trying to compensate for their visual, phonological and/or auditory processing difficulties. This will invariably make them slower. When you hear them read, they often seem more like a beginner reader. It is as though they are continually trying to decode whole words by breaking them down into parts. As you can imagine, this can be extremely mentally exhausting.

Author Alert

This fact alone brings to light a critical factor which will affect the lives of dyslexic children every day.

> **"It will always be extremely hard for skilled, automatic readers to imagine what it must be like to not be able to read and process words easily. Non-dyslexics will often assume that the real problem is a lack of intelligence, effort, stubbornness, laziness or a disinterest in learning altogether. Some even believe that a struggling child's parents are too proud and are unable to recognise, or won't admit, that their child may not be as smart as they think."**

This inability to recognise a struggling learner can also apply unfortunately to the parents and the teachers of dyslexic children.

> **"Keep this thought in mind though: the day your child started school, they fully intended to achieve personal success and make you proud of them. There is a good chance it never entered their mind that they would struggle to learn and on some days even fail."**

Who Is Sally Shaywitz And What Does Brain Imaging Show Us?

Sally Shaywitz MD, is also a world renowned leading expert on the study of dyslexia. She is a neuroscientist and Professor of paediatrics at Yale, in New Haven, Connecticut, America. Sally Shaywitz, along with her collaborators, specialises in watching brains while they read and process language using functional magnetic resonance imaging (fMRI). In her research studies she has discovered that many dyslexics use differing parts of their brain to process language and decode letter symbols into words.

Sally Shaywitz has used fMRI to scan several thousand children and adults as they read or attempt to read. This sophisticated software allows for the capture of brain blood flow images; blood flow tells you which parts of the brain are most active during different tasks.

These fMRI scans have demonstrated three neural systems for reading in the brain: one for fluency, another for word analysis and one for word form. These are generally found on the left side of the brain in a non-impaired reader.

A dyslexic brain differs and there appears to be a disruption to two of the neural systems; one which appears to be responsible for the critical word form area and the other which allows for rapid, fluent and automatic reading. The remaining word analysis area though appears to be overactive. This discovery is common to many dyslexics and has become known as the neural signature for dyslexics.

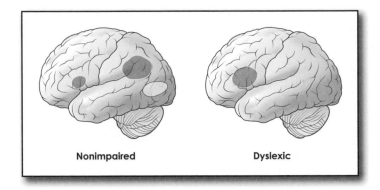

Nonimpaired   Dyslexic

fMRI scans also reveal that the dyslexic brain compensates for this neural disruption by using other parts of the brain. This can allow for more accurate reading skills to be developed when compared to non-dyslexics, but causes word processing and fluency rates to be affected, which is why dyslexics continue to read slowly. Because our brains are plastic and will compensate for areas of weakness, dyslexics can develop substantial neural systems supporting the memorisation of words to overcome this glitch.

Will Dyslexia Only Affect My Child's Literacy Skills?

By definition dyslexia is a difficulty with language, but in my experience it is highly unusual for dyslexics to have a disability which affects just literacy skills. Remember here that every child is different. No two are ever going to be exactly alike, even within the same family.

It seems the word 'dyslexia' has come to represent a range of learning difficulties. In every book or resource you read, you will always see reference to the definition of dyslexia being related primarily to literacy skills. Alongside literacy, however, a child with dyslexia will commonly have other traits which can affect other school subject areas and skills.

To help specialists identify your child's specific learning disabilities, the most common symptoms, traits and characteristics are described using a range of specialised terms. This range of terms may be unfamiliar to you and can prove confusing as parents go through the process of learning how to understand and support their child. When getting a definite diagnosis and seeking support through your child's school, it is important for you to know the 'lingo' so you can keep up with all that is going on throughout the process. I hope the following diagram will help you to clarify some of the most used specialist terms related to dyslexia.

THE DYSLEXIA UMBRELLA

Developmental Dyslexia – you are born with it

Acquired Dyslexia – develops as a result of damage to the brain

DYSLEXIA

Dys – meaning difficulty
Lexia – to do with language

Ongoing difficulty with reading – Dyslexia

Ongoing difficulty with spelling – Dyslexia

Ongoing difficulty with pronunciation of words – Dysphasia or Apraxia

Ongoing difficulty with handwriting – Dysgraphia

Ongoing difficulty with muscle tone and poor posture – Dyspraxia

Ongoing difficulty with balance, small and large body movements – Dyspraxia

Ongoing difficulty with listening and understanding – Auditory Dyslexia / Auditory processing problems

Ongoing difficulty with attention, memory, recall and response – Executive dysfunction

Ongoing difficulty with organising thoughts, time, materials and belongings – Executive dysfunction

Ongoing difficulty initiating, planning, sequencing and ordering information – Executive dysfunction

Ongoing difficulty with visual perception, spatial relations, orientation and direction – Visual dyslexia / Visual processing problems

Ongoing difficulty with numbers, mathematical symbols, terms and concepts – Dyscalculia

Ongoing difficulty with identifying rhyme and rhythm – Auditory Dyslexia / Auditory processing problems

Chapter 5

Dyslexia research – a simple explanation

Dyslexia Research – A Simple Explanation

I find that the easiest way to describe dyslexia is that your child's brain takes in information, but is slower to react to it, or mixes and scrambles it up. The information that their brain receives can be visual, for example, what they see, or auditory, what they hear. Specialists often refer to it as a phonological, visual or auditory processing problem.

Processing problems affect all of us from time to time. They are part of being human. You may refer to these mix ups as senior moments, brain strain, hitting the pause button, simply misplacing something or forgetting what you had intended to write, say or do next.

Everybody has strengths and weakness in relation to their processing skills. You may have no sense of direction or take hours to get organised to begin a simple task, but you may have excellent ball skills and be able to walk into a crowded room and know exactly what is going on in a matter of seconds. Every skill we possess is a result of our brain's processing capabilities.

Being dyslexic is different. A dyslexic's processing problems are ever present. The effects of this can impact upon an individual every day, every hour and sometimes every minute. The outcome of this can be extreme despair and frustration for your child and it can impact on your family too.

> **"An individual who has a learning disability like dyslexia will demonstrate a repeated pattern of difficulty with learning or performing a particular set of skills over an extended period of time."**

My husband Andrew is a highly intelligent and successful man, but sometimes when I ask him a question, particularly if he is busy, it is common for him pause for what seems like forever before he answers me. When I stare at him impatiently, waiting... waiting... he will point out to me that the thoughts in his head are ordered, and my question was simply put in a queue to be answered when his brain is ready.

In summary, dyslexia is a learning disability that gets in the way of how people receive process and/or express information. It can range from relatively mild to extremely severe and affects a person's ability to process information and their learning outcomes over time.

What Does The Latest Research Tell Us About Dyslexia?

Dyslexia is a real neurobiological disorder. 'Neuro' referring to the brain's nervous system and 'biological' defining the operating structure and systems within our bodies.

Why Are Our Magnocells And Genes So Important?

According to the 'Magnocelluar Theory of Dyslexia' documented in John Stein's work, our nervous system has a large number of magnocellular nerve cells. These constitute a system of large neurons, which are specialised in receiving and processing information. It is believed that large magnocells are responsible for the timing functions within our brains. When our brain receives sight (visual) and sound (auditory) cues for processing, magnocells are responsible for the rapid responses to these cues. They rapidly fire passing information along via our nervous system from our eyes and ears until it reaches the brain and we respond accordingly.

Think of it like turning on a light switch and the light instantly coming on. The conduction of electricity along the electrical cable is similar to the way our nervous system operates when we use our brains to think, talk and read.

John Stein, together with Silvia Paracchini's research indicates that in dyslexics, early brain development is often impaired. Their recent studies indicate a number of possible causes:

- Research indicates the faulty movement and development of these nerve cells during the development of a baby's brain while still in the mother's womb. It seems that some of these cells are incorrectly formed or may move inaccurately, causing them to not connect up as efficiently. They become misplaced in the highly structured layers forming the cerebral cortex, or grey matter. The cerebral cortex is the most distinctive structure of the human brain and is responsible for controlling the higher cognitive functions, such as the ability to speak and read which distinguish us from other animal species.

> **"It is extremely important for people to understand that there are genetic variants associated with dyslexia and these genes are not abnormal."**
>
> Dr. Silvia Paracchini

- Genetic variants on chromosome 6 have been identified with a higher frequency in dyslexics. These variants have been shown to be associated with a reduction in the level of a protein important in guiding nerve cell movements and guiding them to the right place during foetal brain development. A drop in this protein production causes minor brain changes that begin before birth. These changes are thought to contribute to reading problems, including dyslexia.

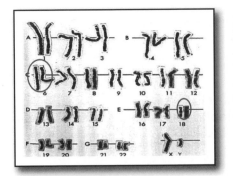
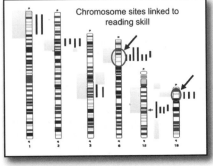

Image Courtesy of Prof. John Stein, Dyslexia Research Trust

Based on research results, Silvia Paracchini proposes that this gene sequence occurs in about 15% of the general population and has also been identified in a large sample of children who have been accurately diagnosed with dyslexia. Its frequency however rises up to 28% in groups of children who have been diagnosed with severe dyslexia. This indicates that the gene sequence is associated with dyslexia and that approximately 15% of the English speaking population carries a risk factor for dyslexia which has been passed down through generations of the same family. It is very likely that when this factor acts in combination with other risk genes or risk environments, the individual will develop dyslexia.

- A recent study was conducted of more than 6000 British children from the general population, aged between seven and nine years of age. Each child was examined and tested on numerous reading and spelling activities. Of all the children tested those who inherited from their biological parent, this particular gene sequence on chromosome 6, tended to perform poorly on tests of reading and spelling abilities, whether or not they had already been classified as dyslexic. It is important to note that, on average, the children with this particular key gene sequence scored as well on intelligence or IQ tests as the other children did.

- Research studies have also identified other candidate genes for dyslexia on chromosomes 3 and 15, while another gene on chromosome 6 has also recently been identified. These genes seem to play a role in guiding the early movement of neurons during brain development.

- John Stein believes that premature babies may also have a tendency to develop dyslexia because of the immature development of their magnocellular neurons at birth.

- A connection between impaired magnocells within the cerebellum, (the brain's autopilot at the back of the brain for controlling movement) and dyspraxia has also been made. Research shows a decrease in the co-ordination and balance of baby mice that have been exposed to the serum from human mothers pregnant with dyslexic children.

- Studies on twins further uncover the role of genetics in having dyslexia and related reading problems. The inheritance of dyslexia in genetically identical twins that share 100% of the same genes is 68%, versus 40% in non-identical twins who share 50% of genes. This indicates that genetics are a strong component, because twins with exactly the same genes tend to develop more consistent reading problems. However, since this rate is not 100%, it indicates that other factors including environment are also having an effect.

- Research also shows a high incidence of auto-immune conditions in dyslexics such as allergies and asthma when compared to non-dyslexics. The reason for this is thought to be that during the pregnancy a mother with dyslexic children develops anti-magnocellular antibodies. These antibodies react with the developing magnocells of the unborn child, possibly impacting on their normal development and decreasing the effectiveness of the surface antigen known as CAT 301. This antigen enables magnocells to connect effectively and efficiently with each other, with one of the suggested outcomes being a high incidence of auto-immune conditions being prevalent in children with dyslexia.

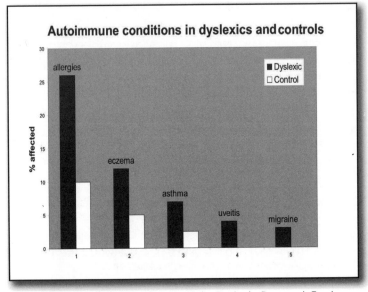

Image Courtesy of Prof. John Stein, Dyslexia Research Trust

John Stein believes that the faulty development and timing of large magnocells can impact on individuals with dyslexia in three ways by affecting visual, auditory and motor skills.

- The visual magnocellular system directs attention and eye movements to identify visual cues such as symbols and their order.

- The auditory magnocellular system tracks auditory cues such as speech frequency and determines the brain's ability to distinguish the distinct units of sounds and their order in the English language.

- The motor magnocellular system determines ability with speaking, writing, balance and co-ordination, etc.

The Role Of Genetics And Family In Having Dyslexia

As you can see there is strong scientific evidence to suggest a genetic link or family history in the prevalence of dyslexia. As in any biological family, traits like eye and hair colour or personality features are passed down through the generations. In some families the fact that dyslexia has been inherited is obvious. Other families report that it skips a generation or moves sideways from an aunt or uncle to a niece or nephew. Genetic scientists are proving critical in providing research results that indicate a genetic link in children with reading difficulties.

Ongoing genetic research has also been critical in helping us to understand more about the prevalence of dyslexia. In the future it could become even more important as it continues to help us to understand what dyslexia is by studying the exact function of genes that indicate a risk for dyslexia. It also offers the future provision of diagnostic testing for the early detection of dyslexia, through genetic screening of children with a family history of dyslexia.

In my experience, some people can remember their childhood vividly and have great insight into how it feels to be a child, while others have little or no memory of it. It is human nature to try to block out memories that are painful and this can be especially true for dyslexics who struggled through childhood and school. Many fail to remember simply because they are dyslexic.

"A struggling child with dyslexia can benefit if they have a close family relative with whom they can confide, talk and relate to."

How Many People Are Dyslexic?

Dyslexia is very common, but how common? I can walk in to a room and mention the word 'dyslexia' and people will invariably relate a story to me about being dyslexic, having the traits, having a child with it or knowing somebody with it.

Yet there can also be a negative stigma or perception of personal weakness attached to having dyslexia in some families, which impacts upon open discussion about the condition. Just because it is never mentioned does not mean it does not exist, it is just not publicly recognised.

After reading 100's of research reports on dyslexia while researching this book, I can tell you that the statistics range from 5% to 20% of the English speaking population. The general rule of thumb for a majority of research studies is 10%. If you do the math, this represents on average one person in ten. Based on this figure you begin to understand why everybody knows somebody with dyslexia.

What Dyslexia Is NOT

It is important to understand that a learning disability like dyslexia is not the same as mental retardation, autism, deafness, blindness or behavioural disorders. However it is possible for children with dyslexia to have more than one disability.

It is thought that Dyslexia, Dypraxia, Attention Deficit Hyperactivity Disorder (ADHD), Executive Dysfunction, Specific Language Impairment (SLI), and The Autistic Spectrum share many features and can be prevalent in generations of the same family. This occurs in the same way that people in the same family can have a range of similar physical characteristics like brown hair, green eyes and freckles.

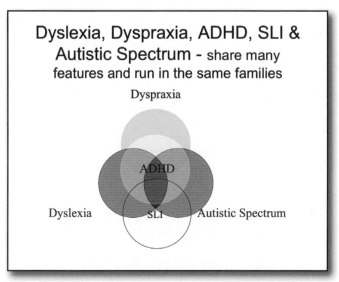

Image Courtesy of Prof. John Stein, Dyslexia Research Trust

Importantly, dyslexia is not seen as an indicator of general intelligence, although many dyslexics are often made to feel that it is. People who suffer from developmental dyslexia are in many cases of normal or above normal intelligence.

For more information on these and other learning disabilities which can relate to dyslexia, visit: DyslexiaDaily.com

An Official Definition Of Dyslexia

For your information, please see the exact definition as adopted by the International Dyslexia Association (IDA) and the National Institute of Child Health and Human Development (NICHHD) USA on the following page. This was adopted by the IDA Board of Directors, November 12, 2002.

"Dyslexia is a specific learning disability that is neurological in origin, characterised by difficulties with accurate and/or fluent word recognition and by poor spelling and decoding abilities. These difficulties typically result from a deficit in the phonological component of language that is often unexpected in relation to other cognitive abilities and the provision of effective classroom instruction. Secondary consequences may include problems in reading comprehension and reduced reading experience that can impede growth of vocabulary and background knowledge."

This was adopted by the IDA Board of Directors, November 12, 2002

There are hundreds of definitions of dyslexia. Of course the best one for you is the one that makes the most sense and allows you to understand exactly what is causing your child's struggle to learn.

A Favourite Definition Of Dyslexia

One of my favourites is this proactive definition taken from Gavin Reid and Shannon Green's book, '*100 Ideas For Supporting Pupils With Dyslexia*'. I would like to see this definition in every teacher staffroom.

"Dyslexia is a processing difference experienced by people of all ages. Often characterized by difficulties in literacy, it can affect other cognitive areas such as memory, speed of processing, time management, co-ordination and directional aspects. There may be visual and phonological difficulties and there is usually some discrepancy in performance in other areas of learning. It is important that individual differences and learning styles are acknowledged since these will affect outcomes of learning and assessment. It is also important to consider the learning and work context as the nature of the difficulties associated with dyslexia may well be more pronounced in some situations."

The Future Of Dyslexia – Can It Be Cured?

fMRI or functional magnetic resonance imaging has provided recent ground-breaking advances in understanding dyslexia. fMRI provides a scan of the brain at work. An individual being scanned will complete a series of language-based tasks. The scanner will then map and record the parts of the brain that are working and doing the thinking. Studies indicate that there are three main neural pathways at work in the brain during reading. There are two for beginner readers who are slowly identifying groups of letter symbols and their associated sounds to gain meaning and one for more competent skilled readers who can recognise familiar words on sight or automatically. All parents and children need to understand that fMRI scans show the brains structure is normal in dyslexics; it is the wiring of nerves or magnocells in the brain that are believed to be the problem.

So to further understand the struggle your child has with processing words for reading, writing and spelling, take this information into consideration. fMRI scans indicate that highly-skilled, non-impaired readers competently use an area at the rear of their brain which enables them to read words automatically from memory. This area of the brain can react in less than 150 milliseconds (less than a heartbeat) to a word once it is learnt and can automatically recognise a group of letter symbols in a particular order as representing known words. Skilled readers therefore speed through their reading tasks, instantly recognising one word after another.

It's in this important section at the rear of the brain that dyslexic children seem to have their problem. The neural pathways are not operating as they should, making automatic word identification and therefore fluent reading very difficult. Studies also indicate that this is true of older children and adults with dyslexia, indicating that a child will not 'grow out' of dyslexia naturally over time without parental and educational intervention.

It seems that dyslexics compensate for this neural break down by relying very heavily on other parts of the brain to read and process information. Unfortunately these are not deemed to be as automatic. When reading, dyslexics seem to rely heavily on those areas that are normally used by beginner readers as they learn words for the first time and analyse them to gain meaning. fMRI studies have shown that even high achieving successful dyslexic students, who read accurately but slowly, also have this trait.

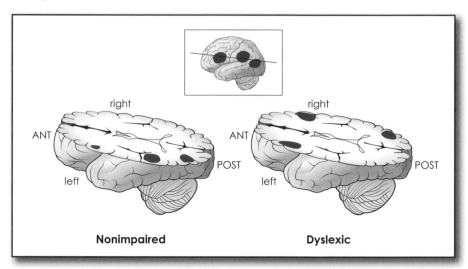

Based on the many studies of competent readers using fMRI conducted in the last 10 years around the world, there is no doubt that dyslexic people use different neural pathways to process words than non-dyslexic readers. This research provides no doubt that the main problem for dyslexic children is in transforming written letters into the appropriate sounds, which is the key to reading. These amazing fMRI images now provide concrete evidence that dyslexia is a physical condition that causes difficulty with reading and processing information. The images also provide the proof to explain how young dyslexic adults can read accurately but slowly with practice, relying on different neural pathways within their brains.

It is now possible, through the use of fMRI scans, to identify different types of dyslexic processing and reading difficulties. It is important to remember that no two children with dyslexia will be identical. Every child with dyslexia has a particular set of factors that impact upon them individually and their ability to decode letter and number symbols for reading, spelling, writing and math.

The most exciting outcome of this research for struggling readers is that dyslexia is becoming less of a mystery. Studies using fMRI scans continue to provide new information to help parents help their dyslexic children. These amazing scans can assess the effectiveness of the reading programs your child is being exposed to. It is important to understand whether the reading program your child is using reinforces pre-existing dyslexic neural pathways within your child's brain, or whether the program is encouraging the development of your child's brain and rewiring it to resemble that of a non-dyslexic automatic reader.

According to studies being conducted around the world to assess whether a dyslexic child's brain can be rewired, the outlook is extremely positive. There are numerous studies to date indicationg that if dyslexia is diagnosed early enough and a child is offered access to scientifically proven literacy programs, research results show that not only can a dyslexic child's brain be rewired, but with ongoing effort and repetition of specific learning tasks, they can begin to resemble those of non-dyslexic children. Dr. Sally Shaywitz's research indicates that there are also great opportunities for the rewiring of brains in older children and adults with dyslexia. In other words, brain repairs are possible and automatic reading methods can be developed.

There are however two critical factors required to make this happen. These are the ability for your child to access evidence based, scientifically proven literacy programs and also your child's level of motivation and commitment to engage in the specific learning tasks that provide the opportunity to rewire their brains to overcome dyslexia.

Go to DyslexiaDaily.com to find an educational program that is suitable for your child or student.

Chapter 6

My child is dyslexic.
How does it feel to be Dyslexic?

Why You Need To Gain A Greater Understanding Of Your Child With Dyslexia

Having a definite diagnosis or a greater knowledge of your child's learning disability is the beginning of your journey to a place called 'true understanding'. It is through this true understanding of what dyslexia is and what it means for your child, that you will become your child's most important ally.

Think of yourself as their manager or representative if this helps. Your child needs your ongoing support and when they begin to realise that you are making a commitment to understand and support them, you will see a positive change in their outlook.

Every parent has the choice to make it their priority to find a way to support their dyslexic child. Empowered parents are a force to be reckoned with, especially when they are educated, level headed and understand what is required to help their dyslexic child to learn and to be successful at school and in life.

> **"As parents, we are in control of our children's destiny. If we can unlock the door to our child's dyslexia, have a firm belief from day one that our child can and will be successful, then there is little doubt that they will be."**

It is never too late to start this journey. This may mean supporting your child as they begin their journey through school or correcting past educational and personal wrongs. Start right now; it is the best time ever for your dyslexic child.

So if you already have your child's diagnostic report or are still raising the funds to pay for your assessment, your struggling child needs you. Right now is the best time to start to understand your child, work with them, and advocate on their behalf. This book will help you to understand your dyslexic child, their potential strengths and weaknesses and how being dyslexic can make them feel.

What Is A Compensated Dyslexic?

The genetic research tells us that it is highly possible that many of the parents reading this book are also language challenged and may be dyslexic too. Are you familiar with the term, 'compensated dyslexic'? This is a person who has lived their entire life with dyslexia, managing to get by regardless of their learning disability. Maybe you are one of these people. If so this book will help you too. Even if you are not dyslexic, it is important to understand what it means so you can really relate to your child.

Is Dyslexia A Gift?

Some people will go so far as to describe dyslexia as a gift. Only an adult could describe it in this way. I can tell you without doubt that if you asked a struggling child on any given day what they thought about being dyslexic, they would tell you it is the bane of their existence, because it makes life, school and learning harder than it needs to be.

The research tells us that dyslexic brains work very hard to process information. fMRI scans show that many more parts of the dyslexic brain are working when you compare them to a non-dyslexic brain completing similar tasks. Perhaps it is this diversity of the dyslexic brain that leads to a diverse range of strengths and advantages, which people can refer to as a gift.

> **"I almost flunked first grade and also the second, third, fourth, and fifth; but my younger brother was in the grade behind me and he was a brain and nobody wanted to have me be in the same grade as him, so they kept passing me. I never learned how to spell, graduated from eighth grade counting on my fingers to do simple addition, and in general was not a resounding academic success."**
>
> *Robert Munsch – Top selling Canadian children's author who wrote 'Love You Forever.' This is one of my all-time favourite children's books.*

The Burden Of Being Dyslexic

There is no doubt about it: growing up and coping with formal schooling when you are dyslexic or struggling to learn can be extremely difficult. There is always a time delay before a learning disability is uncovered and support is forthcoming. The school system in place is designed for more academic, non-dyslexic learners and it also appears there is a lack of general understanding amongst teachers. To top this off there is also a lack of readily available resources in most of our schools for our children.

When you look at it like this, a child with dyslexia has much to bear. If you are the parent or carer of a child with dyslexia, I am sure you will have seen firsthand the difficulties your child has faced, the outcomes of these difficulties and how your child is developing in response to them. Every parent has a different story to tell. At one end of the spectrum these stories are hopeful, incredible dyslexic success stories. At the other end the stories are of lives filled with hardship, some of which have sad and tragic consequences.

> **"The National Literacy Trust conducted the Basic Skills Agency Test on all men incarcerated in UK jails in 1998. This test equates to the reading skills of a 9-10 year old. The results indicated that 60% had problems with literacy and 40% of those had severe literacy problems. Similarly, the Social Exclusion Unit conducted literacy tests in 2002 and discovered that 80% of male prisoners in UK jails had writing skills at or below the expected level of an 11 year old child and the equivalent figures for reading were 50%."**
>
> *Prof. John Stein, FRCP,*
> *Oxford University London*

Always consider that educated parents of children with dyslexia everywhere have a responsibility to try to offer support to other parents of children who are struggling at school. Perhaps this way there will be less tragic outcomes and more success stories. Keep this thought in mind as you develop your own skills and knowledge to help your child.

In time, we may be able to help other parents to help their children. This is the main reason this book came about.

A Point To Ponder

In order to be successful a child must feel success

To contribute to society they must feel like they have something to give

To do what's right they must be recognised for their efforts

If schools and parents provided this for every child perhaps our jails would be empty

Liz Dunoon

How Being Dyslexic Can Make A Child Feel

The impact of being dyslexic can be huge. It can manifest itself in many ways. It is important for parents and carers to realise that they can greatly influence how their child copes with dyslexia, simply by taking an interest in their child and understanding how they can help them to succeed.

The following list is a rather unhappy one, but it is important for parents to be aware of how a dyslexic child with or without support can feel on any given day. It can be so frustrating that many children will eventually consider giving up, becoming invisible, wreaking havoc, running away or just feel like dying inside.

I am sure many of you will relate to the following list of how being dyslexic can make your child feel.

- Different
- Not normal
- Alone

- Frustrated
- Angry
- Sad
- Embarrassed
- Lost
- Annoyed
- Jealous
- Exhausted
- Cheated
- Dumb
- Stupid
- Terrorised
- Bullied
- Nervous
- Panicked
- Full of dread
- Sick
- Exposed
- Discouraged
- Why me?
- Limited
- Overwhelmed
- Inadequate
- Inferior
- Isolated
- Lonely
- Depressed
- Worthless

This list could be endless and I'm sure you could add to it. Even with your unwavering support, your dyslexic child will have days when they feel like life is incredibly unfair as they compare themselves to other children around them who seem to breeze through the school day with little or no effort.

Although dyslexia is invisible, your child may also feel at times as though they are a big loser and surely everybody can see it just by looking at them. It can just be so frustrating to suffer with dyslexia while you are in the school education system.

To survive these constant feelings of inadequacy, your child needs you and an educated, confidence building support team around them to help them cope with the social aspects of school and to really thrive in this structured, book based, academic environment.

> **"Since I was stupidest kid in the class, it never occurred to me to try to be perfect, so I've always been happy as a writer just to entertain myself. That's an easier place to start."**
>
> *Stephen J Cannell, prolific screenwriter, producer and director*

So What's Good About Being Dyslexic?

Firstly, we all need to be aware that having dyslexia can and does provide advantages. That's right, I said advantages. There are skills that some dyslexic people excel in that many non-dyslexics do not. Maybe you can recognise some of these strengths in your own child or maybe even yourself.

Dyslexics may have or can develop the following:

Physical strengths

- Be equally capable with both the right and left sides of their bodies or may be extremely dominant on only one side to a high level of skill.
- May have incredible energy levels.
- May excel in physical skills and as a result be incredibly capable sports people.
- May have exceptional reflexes and be able to respond to physical stimuli almost instantly.
- May have excellent hearing, often hearing sounds moments before others are aware. *'I can never mutter under my breath when my son is around, he always hears it.'*
- Can be amazing singers, mimics or musicians.
- Are often incredible movers, gymnasts or dancers.
- May have excellent dexterity leading to high-level computer keyboarding, piano, organ or accordion skills.
- Can have high physical endurance levels.

Personality strengths

- Can be excellent communicators, making them extremely popular amongst their peers.
- Are often fantastic organisers who efficiently organise people and tasks to get things done.
- Can be great delegators, ensuring that projects are completed in a timely fashion by choosing the right people to complete certain tasks.
- Can be incredible orators, able to speak, recite and perform with great skill while keeping everybody's attention.
- May be incredibly quick witted and funny with words.
- May be able to effectively explain, describe or communicate instructions, ideas or information to others.

- Are often outwardly thoughtful, caring and empathetic towards other people and animals in need.

> **"I had to train myself to focus my attention. I became very visual and learned how to create mental images in order to comprehend what I read."**
>
> *Tom Cruise, Actor*

Mental strengths

- May have a very high pain tolerance.
- Can have incredible mental perseverance, never giving up until they achieve their goals.
- Are often extremely inquisitive, asking thousands of questions about the world and wanting to know how everything works.
- Can achieve great success overcoming obstacles, long after everyone else has given up and gone home.
- Are often fantastic at memorising long paragraphs of written text, verses, songs, poetry, speeches, or lines for a play, etc.
- May possess an amazing understanding of mechanics, electronics or computers.
- Can often be found in kitchens concocting and inventing amazing dishes.
- May be excellent at math and able to think in numbers making them incredible mathematicians and statisticians.
- Can sometimes use their imagination to tell amazingly, detailed and descriptive stories.
- May have a very ordered mind, enabling them to take in large amounts of information, retain this knowledge and then apply it to other areas of knowledge or tasks.

- May be big picture people, able to use high-level strategy, management and delegation skills to reach favourable outcomes.

Visual strengths

- Can often visualise in three dimensions, from different directions and from multiple aspects, making them excellent inventors, planners, engineers, designers, architects, builders and overall creators.
- Can see incredible detail in the world around them, giving them an appreciation of their surroundings.
- Are often able to see the world in an amazing spectrum of colours.
- Can be fabulous artists or photographers.
- Are often incredibly talented at sports where hand-eye and foot-eye coordination are required, such as ball games.

Business strengths

- If you look through this list it doesn't take long to realise that dyslexic people can have incredible skills and talents giving them advantages, which non-dyslexics may not possess. This can make them exceptional employees in the right job, and incredible business people in their own right.

"Encourage your dyslexic child to aim high - there is no reason why they shouldn't. There are ways to achieve greatness. You can inspire your child to dream and to find them."

Don't be disheartened if you cannot see any of these strengths in your child just yet. Watch them closely when you can. Sometimes your child is putting so much effort into trying to cope with school and meeting learning benchmarks, there is no time or energy left to enable them to develop or display their true talents. It is often after formal schooling is completed that individuals with dyslexia begin to shine.

Learning to live with dyslexia is a learning process in itself and with your help your child's brain will eventually develop and find a way to succeed. With you on their team they will have the confidence to find their strengths and their developing brain will help them to excel.

Are you wondering where this list came from?

- Personal observation and interviews
- Directly from word of mouth accounts of parents of children with dyslexia
- From teachers who teach or have taught children with dyslexia
- From verbal accounts of adults with dyslexia, many of whom are now highly successful
- From employers who prefer to employ people with dyslexia
- From tertiary educational institutions who recognise and have direct contact with students with dyslexia

If you start to do your own personal research, as I did, you will be able to identify with this list of strengths and maybe even add to it. When you meet someone who indicates they may have dyslexia, ask them what they are really good at. There is always an answer. Those individuals who have capitalised on their strengths invariably end up extremely successful.

Incredibly Successful And Famous Dyslexics

There are amazing people all around us who have learned to live with dyslexia. There is virtually no job that dyslexics cannot do and if you ask around you may find some great role models for your child, or even a potential mentor. Some of these people are public figures your child may even have heard of. These famous, highly successful dyslexics can motivate, inspire and instil confidence in your child. For this reason your child needs to know all about these people so they can see the possibilities and imagine a positive future even though they are dyslexic.

Go to DyslexiaDaily.com and you will find a list of famous dyslexics and their quotes. Make sure your child is aware of it.

Stay Focused On Your Child's Strengths

By the time you reach the end of this chapter you will probably have mixed emotions.

On one hand, I have emphasised all the emotional turmoil your child can experience in their daily struggle at school. On the other, I have highlighted many of the strengths that can come from being dyslexic. I want you to remember that the aim of this book is to give you the hope and courage to begin your dyslexic education and help your child. So stay focused on all that is positive. The next chapter is fun. It challenges you to spend some time considering what may be going on in your dyslexic child's mind.

Carol Greider is a Molecular Biologist and was the Winner of the 2009 Nobel Prize For Medicine. These are her comments on her application to attend university.

"My application package was a bit unusual", Greider says. "I had great research experience, great letters of recommendation, and outstanding grades, but I had poor GREs."(Standardised secondary school test results).

"Although she did not know it growing up, Greider suffers from dyslexia, which affected her scores on standardised tests. Only two schools—the California Institute of Technology (Pasadena, CA) and the University of California, Berkeley— offered her an interview."

Chapter 7

Are you ready for the dyslexia challenge?

How Does My Child With Dyslexia Feel?

Of course the only way to really understand what it feels like to be dyslexic, is to actually be dyslexic. Many parents and family members reading this book may be experts in this field because they too are dyslexic, but this is not always the case. Here are some ways to help you to understand the daily challenges that your child may face and also an opportunity to experience how your child may think.

Slip inside your child's dyslexic mind as you consider the following tasks.

Language Processing Challenges

1. The Thinking Challenge

Have a conversation with a friend where you are not allowed to use the words 'the', 'and' or 'a'. Make it a conversation that lasts for at least five minutes. What this will do is make your brain continually think ahead to decide what you are going to say to make your conversation meaningful. Without being able to use these important little words, you will begin to speak slower. After five minutes, if you try to keep going your brain will begin to scramble and you will begin to feel exhausted.

This is how your child with dyslexia can feel all day as they try to talk, read, spell, answer questions and recall information from their memory. Their brains are working overtime, but if we are watching them they can appear to be working in slow motion as they constantly process and search for the right words to say. Processing language can be extremely slow, difficult and tiring for dyslexics and this can be an all day, every day event.

2. The Spelling Challenge

Can you tell whether the following names are spelt correctly?

Catriona, Zachariah, Siobhan, Maeve, Stephen, Bartholomew, Xavier, Andreas, Jacqueline.

Choose a name you do not know how to spell. Now imagine you are writing a letter to apply for your dream job. The letter must be posted in the next five minutes to catch today's mail and whether your application is accepted or not will be determined by whether you know the correct spelling of the name of the Human Resources Officer. Where do you look? Is it on the internet or in the newspaper? Who can you ask? Do you ring someone? Do you have an old baby name book? Can you find it written somewhere in time? Proper names are not in the dictionary and are often difficult to find. Take a note of the time it takes you to check the spelling. Did you get anxious, frustrated and panicky?

Spelling is not a strong point for most dyslexics as words are often not easily stored in their memory and are therefore difficult to recall automatically. This can make them slow to write, complete class work and related writing tasks. Other children can learn spelling words long enough to do well on a test, but won't be able to retain them permanently. Being a struggling speller is often time consuming and frustrating, which can greatly limit your child's output of written work and often their success on written spelling tests. Remember though, the words are usually there; they just can't always accurately retrieve them when they need to use them.

3. The Public Speaking Challenge

How do you feel about public speaking? Imagine you are going to hear a famous scientist speak about the effects of global warming, greenhouse gas emissions and carbon trading. You arrive at the lecture hall and there are 1500 people in the audience, including television crews and the media, waiting for this ground breaking speech to start.

Suddenly, an official walks up to where you are seated and tells you quietly that the speaker has fallen ill and that you have been chosen to replace them. You walk up the steps and on to the stage in front of the huge, expectant crowd. Massive overhead spotlights blind you. You look down at the written notes on the lectern, realising that the print is tiny; you cannot even pronounce some of the scientific words. You are so nervous you are shaking, your mouth has gone dry and no words will come out. It's like a bad dream.

This is often how your dyslexic child will feel when they are asked to read in public – absolute dread. Reading aloud can create huge amounts of anxiety and stress, even more so when there is no opportunity to mentally prepare or practise. Even if your dyslexic child is a reasonable reader, the stress of reading in public can cause your child to have an internal melt down, resulting in a panic attack.

4. The Listening, Understanding And Responding Challenge

Watch a foreign movie on television without the subtitles, or hire a foreign movie from the DVD shop. At the end of the movie, imagine you are going to be asked twenty questions about the story, some related to factual information and some related to the outcomes of the storyline and how this film relates to modern society. You watch the movie, but you can't understand the language, or even follow the story. Can you tell what the movie is about? Did you zone out from listening to the language spoken? What else did you look at while watching the foreign movie to help you figure out what was going on?

Dyslexic children often get lost in classroom, family and social conversations as they struggle with the speed required to process all the words and instructions. When language becomes scrambled and blurry, dyslexic children will often use other methods to gain meaning, such as visual cues like facial expressions, setting, tone of voice used, watching responses of others and guessing. Quite often they can get the gist of what is expected of them in terms of a response or an action, but understandably the detail can be lost. It's a bit like listening to a joke which you don't really understand, and then laughing inappropriately at the wrong time. When your dyslexic child responds inappropriately to any given situation it may be that they have been unable to process the language in the lead up to their response.

5. The Performance Challenge

When we are tired and unwell or we have someone looking over our shoulder, our writing or typing skills can suffer. This is a temporary condition and as we rest and recover or the stress of being watched is removed, our skills improve dramatically. To really understand how it feels to be dyslexic, you need to sit on your favourite writing hand and use only your non-dominant hand to type or write for a whole day. Your writing will become irregular, you will have trouble staying on the lines and you will get the letters around the wrong way as you try to increase your speed. More mistakes will creep in as the day goes on and the eraser and the white out will become your best friend. How would your friends, family and workmates respond to your attempts to write?

Many dyslexic children are renowned for having clumsy, irregular handwriting with much overwriting and crossings out. The effort required to write perfectly can be enormous when you are dyslexic and it can take large amounts of time to complete writing tasks. The dyslexic child can often see that their writing is not meeting the classroom standards, but is unable to control the pen or pencil quickly enough to keep up with the other students. It can be extremely frustrating when other children seem to be able to do this with little effort, making many dyslexic children feel inadequate. Even though they are trying their hardest, students and teachers often tell them their writing is not good enough. Because of this, it is common for many dyslexic children to stop trying and they begin to avoid writing tasks completely, often producing very little written work.

6. The Taking Notes Challenge

Find a passage in Greek, Russian or Chinese and set your timer for five minutes. Copy the foreign language as accurately as you can onto a new piece of lined paper. How well did you do? Ask a friend to assess your efforts and give you a mark out of ten. Another great exercise to try is to copy a passage written in English, but you have to write it completely upside down in mirror image from right to left.

I can imagine you had to contemplate each symbol as a separate entity and check it's accuracy before you could move onto the next. Am I correct? Copying from the blackboard, the whiteboard, from the computer or from textbooks can be very slow and laborious for children with dyslexia. Sometimes the meaning of the words gets lost as they copy letter for letter or word part for word part. Not an effective way to record meaningful information or to learn and retain spelling patterns in unknown words. Children will often rush to keep up with their peers when copying, making the formation of letters incorrect and the writing untidy.

Mathematical Processing Challenges

1. The Accuracy Challenge

Look at this address for just three second and then place your hand over it. Write it down on a scrap piece of paper. Check your accuracy.

*5976 Old Maroondah Road, Chesburg,
Williamsdale County BDN 98632.*

How accurate were you with the numbers? Did you mix some of them up?

Look at this mobile phone number for just three seconds and then place you hand over it. Write it down. Check your accuracy.

0421 951 745

How accurate were you with the numbers? Did you substitute some of them or mix them up?

Just about everyone can remember a time in their schooling when a mathematical task was difficult and challenging, no matter how good at maths they were. For dyslexics, the difficulty is often created when they try to recall the exact order of a number accurately. It is not that they don't know the number or can't see the number accurately, it is that on the way to being processed and memorised by the brain, the numbers can become mixed up. This can result in numbers being recalled wrongly and written down incorrectly.

Even when your child knows the correct answer verbally to a maths problem, they can write the answer incorrectly. As a dyslexic child becomes aware of this fault, they can appear slow to complete their maths work as they double and triple check their work for accuracy. This trait can cause errors in many maths tasks, but particularly in those where there is an instant written response required, such as in mental maths, where children have to write answers to a set number of maths questions within a short time limit.

2. The Writing Wrong Answers Challenge

Try using your own name, but then substituting your friend's child's details when filling out a medical form at the doctors. I'm sure you know some of the answers, but not the details, including heath care numbers, weight, height and whether they have allergies.

When you go into a bank to cash a cheque, try writing your own name on a cheque, but then write the number of your best friend's account. See what happens when you try to cash it.

Obviously you would never do these things, but if you tried to hand the form and cheque in, imagine the look of uncertainty on the bank clerk's face as they realise that the information you have provided is completely incorrect. They may make you feel stupid and assume you are ill or even dishonest.

Writing numbers and facts to fill out class work sheets and complete tests are common occurrences in a child's school day. Confusing numbers, letter and symbols means answers can be written down incorrectly. It can be frustrating, annoying and embarrassing, when children know the correct answers in their head, but cannot retrieve them and write them accurately on the spot.

3. The Using Memory For Action Challenge

Drive down a street you don't know and try to find the house or building at number 231. Did it exist? Did you have any difficulty locating it? Did you need to ask for someone's help? Did they look at you strangely because maybe it didn't even exist?

Dyslexic children often mix up numbers and can find themselves in the wrong place at the wrong time. They may be searching for a bus number, trying to call a phone number, getting you to drive them to an address or trying to find a locker number or a classroom that doesn't even exist. They can feel sure they know the number or have written it correctly, but cannot find it. They end up feeling disorientated, frustrated and confused. The outcomes of these simple errors can be varied. They not only waste valuable time, they may even get into trouble with a parent, teacher or friend for taking too long to complete a seemingly simple task, for being late or for missing an event altogether.

4. The Symbol Challenge

For this maths exercise the following symbols have been altered.

+ Looks like this □

− Looks like this ◆

x Looks like this Δ

÷ Looks like this /

Now do these sums quickly in your head:

4 Δ 3 =

10 □ 12 =

25 ◆ 6 =

35 / 7 =

11 Δ 2 =

6 □ 7 =

12 ◆ 5 =

24 / 6 =

How did you go? How long did it take you to figure out which symbol was which in these simple sums? Such a seemingly simple task - I bet you could do these easily if the symbols were not unfamiliar.

Dyslexic children often mix up simple mathematical symbols and not just these ones. Think how many symbols there are in maths with time, fractions, less than and greater than, decimal places, measurement, algebra and geometry. The list is even longer if you take into account all the symbols we use at school and in life. Symbols can be prone to confusion in a dyslexic child's mind. There is no doubt some of spatial mathematic concepts are also difficult for some dyslexic children to grasp, but always ensure you take into account that a wrong answer can be a simple case of symbols being mixed up.

5. The Tables Challenge

Do you remember the periodic elements table from secondary school science? Can you write down the symbol for oxygen and water? I bet you can remember those two. How about sulphur, magnesium, gold and copper? Maybe! I'll bet you can't remember beryllium, krypton or vanadium.

Learning times tables can be very difficult for dyslexic children and recalling the answers on any given day can be even more of a struggle. The answer to 6x7 was easy to remember yesterday, but cannot be recalled today during a test. Times tables are seen as something that children are meant to know and recall automatically. Some dyslexic children will eventually learn them with your help, but others will always struggle. This can be made even more difficult when some schools now teach mathematics using a whole maths meaningful approach. This method does not allow for any rote learning or repetition to assist with brain training and memory retention.

Processing Information Challenges

1. The Listening For Detail Challenge

Remember back to a time when you were on an important phone call and at the same time somebody was trying to tell you something just as important. Could you juggle both conversations? Could you listen to all the information and respond accordingly to what both people were telling you? Did you get alarmed and annoyed while trying to work out which person to deal with first, the one on the phone or the one standing in front of you?

Dyslexic children are often bamboozled by too much information and too many instructions being given to them at the one time. This is again a processing difficulty and in family homes, classrooms and on the sporting field there can be too much noise and information or too many instructions bombarding your dyslexic child at the same time for them to learn and understand what they are required to do.

2. The Reading For Meaning Challenge

Pick up a newspaper and choose an article. Read the headline and then read only every second paragraph. Do you know what the article is about? Did you miss any of the facts? Could you recount this news story to a friend accurately?

Often dyslexic children have trouble following a story or gaining the full meaning from written text. This means that they may not be able to give a meaningful account of what they have read or answer detailed comprehension questions accurately.

3. The Calling Out The Wrong Answer Challenge

Next time you are driving along in the car, try this little exercise. Call out some obviously incorrect facts while appearing serious. Read the speed signs incorrectly and call out 80 instead of 100, confuse the make of the car in front of you and say it's a Hyundai when it's obviously a Honda, read the name of a café incorrectly and call it 'The Hunchback' instead of the 'Lunch Shack'. Make a note of how people respond to your errors. I'll bet they can't wait to tell you that you are wrong and look at you as though you are mad. They may even tell you that you need to have your eyes checked.

Dyslexic children often make these types of processing errors. By calling out an answer or just answering teacher's questions, they are sometimes putting themselves in a position where they can be ridiculed by those around them. Imagine the child who has just spent precious minutes concentrating really hard and working out the answer to a maths problem, just as the teacher calls out the next maths problem. The child, not realising that the moment has passed, puts their hand up and gives the answer to the previous question, which is accurate, but now out of context. All the children giggle and the child feels embarrassed and humiliated.

You can understand when this has happened on a number of occasions, why children with dyslexia can become very withdrawn and quiet class members. Children with dyslexia may very well know the answers to a teacher's question, but will not risk embarrassing themselves in case they make a mistake. These children may instead respond with an obviously incorrect or humorous answer to make the class laugh. This will ensure that the teacher directs their attention elsewhere.

4. The Thinking On The Spot Challenge

Pick up a pen and a notepad. You have five minutes to write an explanation of how an epidural works. Go to it. After the five minutes is up, you must stop writing with no changes to be made after the time allocated. How did you do? As long as you are not a medical doctor or a nurse, I'm sure you found this task challenging. Does your explanation make sense? Did you write it in a logical order? What would a medical doctor say if you showed it to them? What would they give you as a mark out of ten for your attempt?

Regardless of how much preparation a dyslexic student does, it is still possible that when they sit down to write, their thoughts are completely disorganised. They may know all the names of people and items that relate to their topic, but be unable to remember them when writing. They may know what they need to say, but be unable to structure it into a meaningful order with a beginning, middle and an ending.

5. The Here Today Gone Tomorrow Challenge

If you are a male, look in the mirror and shave half of your whiskers. If you are female put eye makeup on only one eye. Now shut both your eyes and have a go at doing the other side of your face without being able to see what you are doing. What was once a simple task and required little thought now becomes a challenge as you rely upon your other senses to attempt these tasks. I'm sure if you actually did this you would probably look very strange.

Dyslexic children can seem to be processing information effectively and accurately when completing a set task and then at another moment in time seem unable to complete the same task with the same level of processing skill. This inconsistency may seem unusual, but every dyslexic child is different. Many factors can cause this to occur, including the time of day, how much sleep a child has had, the way in which information or instructions are given, the teacher, mental exhaustion and other distractions in the environment such as noise or lighting.

Spatial Skills And Order Challenges

1. The Sense Of Direction Challenge

How is your natural sense of direction? Consider these tasks. Take a walk in your neighbourhood. Every time you reach a place where two roads meet, go left for the first two times and then right for the next two times. Did you get home using this method? How long did it take you? Did you want to go a certain way to get home only to discover you couldn't or you would be breaking the rules?

Have you ever been in an unfamiliar shopping mall? You can start to wander and then discover you are lost. How long did it take you to find your way out again? Maybe you have lost your car in a car park at a concert or sporting event. How did that make you feel?

Dyslexic children are often challenged by direction. This again is a processing problem which can result in an uncertainty of which way they should go. It can be as obvious as confusion with left and right, or more complex as children struggle to find their way to seemingly familiar places like the local shop or even the school office.

This confusion and lack of natural direction can make a dyslexic child lose confidence and become reluctant to venture out. When they do, they will often need to concentrate very carefully on every decision they make to navigate accurately to get to a particular place.

2. The Create Daily Chaos Challenge

Get a small note pad out and write a down all the things you need to do before you leave for work each morning. Make sure you write each task on a different sheet of notepad. Now tear them off the pad and mix them up. Could you follow your new sequence of events? How would you feel about going outside to get the newspapers in your pyjamas or putting on your make up before you shower or wash your face? It feels very strange to be unable to predict what is going to happen next. It can leave you feeling unprepared for the day ahead and feeling like you have missed or forgotten to do something important.

Dyslexic children often have trouble thinking through and prioritising the order of a series of events, or knowing what they need to do next when performing daily tasks or following school routines. This difficulty can make them seem disorganised, pressured, mixed up, slow and confused.

3. The Disorganised Filing System

Imagine taking all your bills for the year out of your filing system, throwing them in the air, collecting them back up and then filing them again randomly. How long would it take to find your credit card bill for last month or to find your electricity bills for the last six months so you can compare the charges? It may take time to find this information and would be rather annoying to have to go through this process to find what you are looking for. Maybe some of you just keep all your bills for the year in one big pile and go through this sorting process at the end of every year.

Dyslexic children often have difficulty mentally locating information from their memory when it is required. The other side of this processing difficulty is that your dyslexic child may also have difficulty storing information practically; this can include writing down information in a logical sequence, or actually storing notes and paperwork correctly, whether it is in a filing system, a folder, on a desktop or in an exercise book. What may not seem too important at the time can later cause all types of stress as your child tries to find a critical piece of information when it is required.

Perception Challenges

1. The Being Ready To Respond Challenge

If, on the spot, you were asked to walk into a lecture theatre filled with 200 students and lecture them about the importance of effective small business accounting, could you do it? Maybe! Maybe not! If you had no idea what to say, would it be a reflection on your intelligence or more likely that you were just totally unprepared.

Dyslexic children often feel like this. Often in life they will be put into a position where they will feel totally out of their depth. This could be when they are called upon to give an answer in class, make an on-the-spot presentation, respond immediately to a request for action or an emergency. It may seem to bystanders that your child is just not clever enough to respond quickly or correctly. Some dyslexic children can also fall into the trap of believing this. It is more likely that they have just been put way out of their comfort zone and are just unprepared for what is expected of them.

2. The Wrong Place - Wrong Time - Help Me Challenge

Have you ever walked into the wrong toilet or walked in on a private meeting or conversation because you were in the wrong place at the wrong time? How did it make you feel? Maybe you have rung the doorbell at the wrong house? Have you ever asked an inappropriate question at school or in a meeting or lecture? Think back to how others reacted to your mistake. What do you think would happen if you always had to ask the person sitting next to you at work to spell words and take notes for you, or even to do your work for you?

Dyslexia is invisible, but this is not the case for your child. It can often cause simple mistakes to occur and can be the reason your child is constantly seeking reassurance and help from you and others, whether it be with their homework or for tasks in general. The answers to your child's constant questions or the reasons for their confusion an and inappropriate behaviour may seem overly obvious to you, but this is not the case for your dyslexic child. Every day you need to consider how you and others react to your child's simple errors, requests for help and reassurance. You need to understand why they continually ask you and others to give them answers to what appears to be overly simple questions. Dyslexic children are often publicly and privately subjected to ridicule, anger, frustration, exasperation, raised eyebrows, silence, sarcasm, hostility and accusations of being slow or stupid or even wasting people's time. Dyslexic children are often mistreated and verbally abused for just being dyslexic. It is important that parents provide support for their child and offer them refuge and relief from this often daily occurrence. The people within your child's social and school network can also be educated to support your child. It is important to remember that having dyslexia is not an indication of a child's intelligence, yet they are often treated with disdain and made to feel that it is.

3. The Starting Over Challenge

Do you remember what it felt like on your first day at a new job? Did you have any doubts about your ability to actually be able to do the job or to fit in with the new people you met? It can feel very unsettling when you begin a new class at night school or walk into a sporting club for the first time as a new member. Sometimes at work we are promoted into new more challenging roles and we have to prove our worthiness to our superiors. Often there is change of ownership or boss in our existing workplace and, as employees, we have to learn to work with and to please our new boss. It can cause us undue anxiety and stress.

Your dyslexic child has to face this challenge every year as they move from one grade level to the next and meet yet another new teacher and often a whole new set of classmates. The support structure that your child has built up during the past year disappears, and not only that, your child also knows that the level of class work will become more difficult and there will be more of it. It is no wonder then that your child may be scared, worried, teary, behaving badly or losing sleep over starting a new school year or maybe even starting at a new school. As parents, we need to be aware of these stresses, how they impact on our child and provide as much support at this time as we can.

How Parents Can Determine The Type Of Adult Their Child With Dyslexia Will Become

Without any support, school years can be a difficult, torrid and dysfunctional time for a dyslexic child. This is directly related to the current education system in which they learn, are tested and assessed. It is a period of time of approximately 12 years from the ages of 5 to 17 years, which must be endured by all dyslexic children. At no other time in their lives will having dyslexia be so challenging and measurable against non-dyslexic children.

Even in colleges and universities today there are often more flexible standards in place to assist those with learning disabilities, depending on their choice of study.

The adult you child will become is a direct reflection of how their childhood, schooling and home life has played out and how confident, capable and successful they will become. In the future as an adult, your dyslexic child will make their own choices, be their own person and live by their own rules.

> **"At the end of the day, all people seek to be accepted and valued for who they are. Your child with dyslexia is no different. They have as much right to be as valued and as successful as all other children and as parents we need to ensure those in positions of power provide our children with these rights."**

As you develop a greater understanding of how being dyslexic can impact your child, you will be better equipped to help them to overcome and manage their learning obstacles and to begin to operate at their full potential.

Chapter 8

My child has been diagnosed with
dyslexia. Should I tell them and
label them?

How To Decide Between 'Yes' And 'No'

When you read this chapter heading, I can almost guarantee that you think you already know the answer to this question. Do you? Was it a definite 'yes' or 'no'? Now I want you to take a moment and ponder why you gave the answer you did.

Let me tell you there is no right or wrong answer, because you have the right to tackle your child's dyslexia in any way you choose. Parents often have strong feelings about whether they should tell their children and label them or not. It is important for you to understand why you feel the way you do.

When you read books or talk to people about dealing with dyslexia, nearly everybody will give you either a 'yes of course you should tell your child' or a 'no, don't subject them to a label for life' point of view based on their age, personal history or education. You will also have developed your view and opinion in the same way.

> **"When you first receive your child's diagnosis, the question of whether to tell them is often the first one you will have to consider."**

Some parents will have already decided before they hear the diagnosis what they are going to say to their child and their family, friends, school and social networks about their child with dyslexia.

For others there can be a degree of uncertainty because they are yet to really understand what it means for their child to be dyslexic and how it is going to impact on their child and everyone else. For a while the jury will be out and after some thinking they will then decide 'yes' or 'no'. There is also the consideration of good timing. It is important to know when the time is right for your child to hear this information. As I said, there is no right or wrong answer, only you can decide what is best for your child.

How you feel about your child being dyslexic is a very critical factor in how you are going to deal with it. The following list is designed to help you to consider what you may be thinking and feeling when you find out, and more importantly, to prompt you to ask yourself why you are feeling this way. Once you have gone through this process and sorted your own feelings out, you can then begin to focus on your child and what is best for them at this time and in the future.

How You May Feel When You Discover Your Child Is Dyslexic

- ° I'm shocked
- ° I'm shattered
- ° I feel so mad... I could scream
- ° I've always known they were dyslexic
- ° I'm gutted, just devastated
- ° I just can't cope with this!
- ° I'm scared and frightened for their future
- ° I feel utter despair
- ° I just feel sick
- ° I'm so worried...what happens now?
- ° I get so teary...I just want to sit in my bedroom and cry
- ° I'm so sad and depressed this is just my worst nightmare
- ° I feel so guilty - why didn't I pick this up before?
- ° I'm so frustrated - how did this happen?
- ° I'm obviously a terrible parent to have allowed this to happen
- ° This can't be happening to me
- ° What will my friends think?
- ° They're OK. We will be fine - it can't be that bad
- ° What do I do now? I'm way out of my depth
- ° I knew there was something wrong and I chose to ignore it - it's my fault entirely
- ° I feel so embarrassed - it's a slight on our good family name

- I'm so jealous - why can't my child be more like......?
- How do I tell my child?
- How do I tell my friends?
- I'm not good at dealing with teachers. They intimidate me and I just clam up
- I don't have the time or the money to deal with this.
- Finally! Now I know for sure, I can understand how to better help my child
- I feel ashamed that I didn't realise there was a problem earlier
- I feel bitter - everything bad happens to me
- I feel angry with my dyslexic child - why can't they just be normal? I've got enough going on already
- I'm angry with my partner – it's all their fault, they bombed out at school too
- I'm angry with my father - this must be inherited - he could never read well either
- I'm angry with myself - I should have been able to work this out for myself years ago and done something about it when I had the chance
- I'm angry with the school - so many years have gone by and my child has never been given the proper assistance and look where we are now
- I feel overwhelmed, not another thing to deal with
- Why didn't my child's teacher at school tell me something was wrong?
- I told those teachers there was something wrong - and they ignored me and told me I was overreacting
- Why didn't I listen to my child's teacher? I could have helped to prevent all this angst
- Now the Education Department has to help my child
- I'm in denial - there's nothing wrong with my child - what are they raving on about?

- ° I feel lost - what do I do now?
- ° I just can't do it - my child will just have to struggle on without me.
- ° Did I do something wrong while I was pregnant?
- ° Maybe it was the difficult birth my child had?
- ° My child was born prematurely - did that have something to do with it?
- ° I should have set a better example, taken more time to read to them when they were little
- ° Whose fault is this? Someone must be to blame
- ° I feel so much better and more in control - now I can get some proper assistance for my child
- ° Great, now my child can access some of the available dyslexic education programs
- ° Finally I have some answers - this is the start of my education to help my child
- ° Relieved - finally I know exactly what is going on
- ° OK! Now I know - let's just get back on with life as we know it

I'm sure you could add many more reactions to this list.

Yes it's true; dyslexia is a challenge, but don't despair. Any learning disability creates challenges and obstacles, but you can help your child overcome them if you understand how.

Life Is Full Of Obstacles And Challenges

Let's face it, as human beings, parents and carers; life is full of challenges and obstacles. Nobody sails through life without having to overcome adversity in one form or another, whether it is obvious to others or not. Humans are complex beings, you only need to scratch the surface and get to know people to realise that we are all dealing with our own personal issues. Never assume a diagnosis of dyslexia is something you cannot deal with.

Dealing With Negative Thoughts And Feelings

Here are some key points to consider if you are feeling unsure and overwhelmed by mixed emotions.

> You are the key and the only key to the door of your child's happiness and success. This book has been written to help you to get started.

> Does it really matter to you or your child's future success if they are labelled as dyslexic or not?

> A label can be private or public, just as any diagnosis can.

> Is a diagnosis of dyslexia a 'label' or a diagnostic report that will enable you to understand in detail why your child struggles to learn?

> If you deny your child a diagnosis, might you also be denying them a prescription for action, as well as access to services, resources and strategies to assist them throughout their formal schooling?

> If having a label is an issue for you, do you allow it to become more important than the actual diagnosis of dyslexia? If so, you need to understand why, and sort out your feelings as quickly as possible.

> Irrespective of the diagnostic report and its findings, as a parent it is up to you to decide, who, when and what you tell your child and other people. It is best to allow your child and their needs to guide you.

> Don't allow your fear of labels to deny your child the opportunity to receive an accurate diagnosis.

> The most important thing to remember is that you need to begin the process of educating yourself and supporting your child with dyslexia as soon as possible. With your help they can and will be a success in life.

Why Love And Good Parenting Is More Important Than Deciding Whether To Label Your Child Or Not

You are a parent or a carer and nothing has changed. You will still do everything you used to do to: love, nurture, care for and provide an education for your child. It's that simple. What is required for your success and ultimately your child's' success is your understanding, understanding how your child learns. By understanding their processing problems, you ultimately unlock their learning strengths and this is the key to the door to helping them succeed at school and in life.

> **"A child will never come to terms with being dyslexic until their parents come to terms with having a dyslexic child."**

If, as a parent, you are still feeling totally overwhelmed by this diagnosis, don't panic, but please seek some help from a trained counsellor or psychologist. Never forget that knowing your child is dyslexic is not the end of the world, but rather an opportunity to provide them with the support they deserve.

Don't Freak Out! Use Your Child's Diagnostic Report To Give You Perspective

When you receive your child's report, sit down and consider it carefully. A diagnosis of dyslexia can be so broad ranging. What does the report specifically tell you about your child's disability? Ask your child's assessor to provide you with a summary of the results on the spot if possible. Write this summary down. The types of processing problems that your child has are not likely to alter greatly in the short term. However with your help, support and specific extra tutoring, your child should improve considerably.

This process of being specific with your child's dyslexia will give you the facts that you require if and when you are ready to provide an explanation to your child about why they struggle and what it means for them. Whether you use the term 'dyslexia' or not is up to you.

If you have decided to tackle the issue of telling your child at a later date because it would be more appropriate, you will again need to familiarise yourself the with the summary of the assessment report. A general classroom teacher will not be able to explain the report results to you as effectively as a qualified dyslexia assessor. Your child's classroom teacher will be way out of their depth, possibly confusing you or providing you with classroom test results, when you really need to understand your child's specific processing problems as described in the report. It is a bit like going to see a general medical practitioner to diagnose cancer when you really need to see a specialist oncologist. You need the facts.

If you received your report some months or years ago, why not ring up the assessor and ask again for the report to be explained in detail? You can make an appointment or ask for an explanation over the phone. The most important thing to remember here is why your child is considered to be dyslexic and more specifically what it means for them.

When and how you tell your child and what you tell them should be a considered process where you take into account the benefits for your individual child.

What You Need To Consider If And When You Decide To Talk To Your Child

> Their age and current level of maturity

> Their current level of understanding about their difficulties to learn

> Their current situation at school and in life

> Their emotional state

> Are they already asking you questions about why they're different to others?

> Why you are going to tell them?

> How are you going to tell them, when, where?

> What words you are going to use to ensure they understand?

> Do you have some examples to use to explain their specific processing problems?

> How do you think they are going to react?

> > What questions might they ask you and have you considered the answers you would give them?

> > What will be the long-term benefits or disadvantages of them knowing?

> > If you tell them will there be any possible negative outcomes?

> > If you have already used the term 'dyslexia' in the past when talking to your child, what else can you tell them to explain and help them further?

A Mother's Decision To Tell – Angela's Story

Lachlan started at the local state primary school when he had just turned six. His mum Angela had held him back a year as he was the eldest child in a family of three and a slow developer. She felt he would benefit from an extra year of growth and maturity before starting school.

On the first day of school Lachlan and his parents were overwhelmed. There was so many students and so many parents and grandparents farewelling them. There must have been close to 100 people in the classroom. Lachlan, a fairly sensitive boy, looked lost. He had tears in his eyes and so did Angela as she left the school grounds that day.

Lachlan settled in well and quickly made some friends and soon began to bring home sight words on flash cards and school readers. It became very obvious very quickly that Lachlan could not read or remember his sight words or read any words in his readers, even after eight weeks of revision and Angela's help. She went in to see Mrs Jones the teacher to seek her opinion. Mrs Jones shocked her. She had absolutely no knowledge that Lachlan was having any trouble at all. There was no system of monitoring the children's progress with their sight words or for the teacher to even hear the children read their readers individually on a regular basis throughout the school term.

Angela decided to continue to assist Lachlan at home, even though he was often mentally exhausted after a day at school. A few months later things were not much better and Lachlan had begun to ask Angela 'Why can't I learn to read like the other kids? It's easy for them and why can they write so good? I can't write fast and neat like them'. Lachlan's dad Alan had struggled at school and Angela began to suspect that Lachlan was going to as well. She again went down to the school to speak to the teacher. Mrs Jones provided lots of excuses for Lachlan's slow development, but did not provide any solutions to her concerns. She did suggest however, that if Lachlan got far enough behind, he might qualify for learning support.

The final straw came a few weeks later when Angela was looking through Lachlan's workbook after school one day and discovered some answers to questions written accurately and relatively neatly. When she questioned Lachlan about this he told her that the boy who sat next to him had helped him by writing in all the answers. He said the boy was kind and had offered to help because he could see that Lachlan was struggling to do his work. Mrs Jones was totally unaware that this had occurred and that it had been occurring on a regular basis. Needless to say, Angela began to look around for a new school.

After speaking to lots of parents and looking through five local schools, she went to one that was 30 minutes' drive away on a personal recommendation. It was a private school that had an excellent learning support program and before she had even selected it they offered to academically assess Lachlan to see which grade level would suit him the best. Five minutes into the assessment, the learning support teacher called Angela aside to ask her if she was aware that Lachlan was dyslexic. 'We can help him,' she said and explained how.

As you can imagine Angela decided to move Lachlan to this school very quickly and as a result Lachlan began an intensive learning support program which saw him begin to improve considerably. Lachlan's mum did not tell him he was dyslexic at that time. He was happy and making good progress, however he still continued to struggle with many aspects of his schoolwork and homework and Angela felt it would be difficult for him to understand. She did however tell him that he learned differently to others and was very like his dad and that he too had struggled at school. She also pointed out that Lachlan's dad was a successful businessman who had done very well despite his struggle at school.

When Lachlan was nine years old and in Grade 3, the schoolwork became harder. Lachlan's school reports were reflecting his learning disability across the board, even with all the extra learning support. Angela never showed him his school reports as they were sent home in the post, but his frustration at struggling more with his schoolwork more than his classmates was becoming constant. Homework was continuing to be a nightmare, filled with anxiety, tension, neediness and defiance. From the moment Lachlan walked in the door it would begin. He would take his mental exhaustion and frustrations out on Angela regularly, which impacted on the entire household and was extremely stressful and wearing.

The learning support teacher continued to be helpful, but Angela wanted to understand Lachlan's learning disability in more depth so she could provide him with more specific assistance. After a day at school Lachlan was mentally exhausted, so she felt she had to provide him with more specific assistance so she didn't waste any of her own crucial time or Lachlan's.

She made an appointment in her nearest capital city to see a specialist dyslexia assessor. I might add that the school's learning support teacher told her that this wasn't necessary and that she was wasting her money, but she persevered. That was in 2007 and it cost her $550.00 dollars and meant a day off school for Lachlan and a day off work for Angela. Angela explained to Lachlan that a special teacher was going to look at how he did his schoolwork and help to explain how he learned. It wasn't a test. There were no right or wrong answers, but it would help her and his teachers to help him with his schoolwork. Although Lachlan was nervous, he knew his mum was on his team and tried to do his best.

All the effort and money spent was worth it. The report was illuminating. It answered all Angela's questions about Lachlan's specific learning problems and told her exactly what she needed to know about his specific processing problems. This enabled her to become more proactive and to offer more appropriate support to her son. A copy of the report was also distributed to his teachers and allowed for special consideration during tests and assessments. Homework and schoolwork was also modified to cater for Lachlan's learning strengths.

As Grade 4 began, again the schoolwork and homework became harder and Lachlan's questions became more persistent. 'Why can't I do the work easily like everyone else at school? What is wrong with me? Why do I always have to try so hard? I get so tired all the time, everybody else breezes through, except for maybe Bridget and John,

I'm better than them.' Angela knew that the day to tell Lachlan that he was dyslexic had finally come. He was ten years old and ready for answers.

"Lachlan," she said, "do you remember when I explained to you that you learn differently from other children and how some things are harder for you than they are for others?"

"Yes," said Lachlan.

"Well there is a reason for it. It has a name. You have a learning disability called dyslexia," said Angela.

Lachlan looked up. "Am I sick? Is it a disease?"

"No," said Angela, "you are perfectly normal and you're not sick".

Lachlan looked confused. "Will I grow out of it? Will it go away? Will I get better?"

"No," said Angela, "but you will learn to live with it and I am always going to be here to help you."

"But how?" asked Lachlan, "I knew there was something wrong with me. I hate being different and having to try so hard all the time". As he said this he began to cry, slowly at first, then he broke into big, heart-wracking sobs, which lasted for a good ten minutes. Angela held her big, strong, beautiful boy in her arms as he sobbed uncontrollably, trying to fight back her own tears, but knowing she had to be strong for him.

Finally he looked up at her with red rimmed eyes and a tear-stained face. "How did I get it? Why me? Why do I have to have this thing? What's it called again?" His voice was breaking again and he was getting desperate now.

"It's called dyslexia," Angela said, "and you were born with it. We can only assume that you've got it because Daddy probably has. It's part of who you are and it explains why you learn the way you do. Do you remember when I took you to see the learning specialist last year? Well she told me about it. She sent me a report. I can show it to you if you like."

"I don't want to see it," said Lachlan in despair.

"Well, if you ever do want to see it, I will show it to you," said Angela. "It explains why you struggle to read, write and spell. Your brain mixes information up. It doesn't mean that you can't do those things or won't ever be good at them; it just means you have to work twenty times harder than everybody else in your class. I think you know that already, don't you? Your brain is actually working harder than everybody else's, that's why you get so tired. The tests showed that you are actually very smart. The report also explains why you mix up numbers and have trouble reading the time, learning your times tables and remembering things. It's all because of your dyslexia."

"So I have dys-dyslec," said Lachlan.

"Dyslexia," corrected Angela.

"And it won't ever go away and I am always going to have to try harder than everybody else, is that right?" asked Lachlan.

"Yes," said Angela.

Finally, Lachlan looked up. "I'm kind of happy in a way," Lachlan said. "I thought I was going crazy. I knew there was something wrong with me."

"No, you're not crazy, you're perfect, you just learn differently to others," said Angela.

"Ok mum, can I go outside now?"

"Of course," said Angela.

After this conversation took place, Angela told me that Lachlan became more peaceful and settled at school and even began to become reflective and insightful. He stopped blaming Angela for his daily struggle and he even began to notice when he was saying and doing things which were a direct result of being dyslexic. He would comment as if it all made sense now and sometimes he could even see the humour in his dyslexic errors.

His favourite two were 'polehunch' instead of 'holepunch' and 'parcark' instead of 'carpark'. It always made him giggle. He began to understand what his weaknesses were and where his strengths lay. He excelled in the area of performing arts and in sport. He started to consciously try harder to keep up with his classmates and use his strengths to define himself. As a direct result his weaknesses were not so dominating and his circle of friends increased as a result of his newfound confidence.

Lachlan is currently in Grade 5 and his schoolwork is still a daily struggle, but Angela tells me he manages to keep up with his peers in class. His report card is usually filled with C's and D's with the occasional B and E, but he continues to move through the school years confidently. He is well aware of the fact that he has to work much harder than everybody else and is proud of himself for never giving up. Now he understands that his tenacity pays off in other areas of his schoolwork and life. Lachlan has also started to think about what he wants to be when he grows up and daydreams about what he could be. Angela continues to tell him he can choose how well he does at school by deciding how hard he wants to work. He is in control of his destiny.

Angela continues to help him by liaising with Lachlan's teachers on a regular basis, making sure he gets all the extra assistance he is entitled to at school.

Angela told me recently that she overheard Lachlan talking while he was outside playing handball with a boy with a mental disability. He said to the boy, "What disability have you got?" The other boy didn't answer and just kept playing handball. Lachlan continued, "It's OK you know. I'm a bit disabled too. I've got a thing called 'dyslexia', which means I have to try much harder than everybody else to learn at school, but it's ok." Angela said it made her so proud that he was growing up to be so self-assured, confident and mature.

A Mother's Decision Not To Tell – Katie's Story

Katie was a mother in the early 1980's, a time when not much was known about dyslexia, how to treat it or how to cope with it. She had very quickly welcomed into the world twin girls just as her husband

Pat was starting a business, an auto mechanic workshop in the outer suburbs of Cardiff in Wales, U.K.

Katie and Pat's twins grew quickly, were highly active and quite a handful. The majority of the home duties were delegated to Katie and their business did very well. However with two active youngsters, Katie was invariably exhausted. Katie and Pat continued to work very hard and were relieved when their children, Beth and Emma finally started school.

Katie had a policy of always being at home before and after school as her children always came first. Pat was rarely home to see the children into bed, but was also a devoted and caring father.

Beth had always been the ringleader of much misadventure and led Emma astray on many occasions. Beth was a free spirited, quick thinker and found the confines of the school classroom very challenging and sitting down to do formal schoolwork almost impossible.

Katie and Pat were often being called up to the school to hear stories of Beth's bad behaviour and her refusal to do much of her schoolwork. The teachers often told Katie and Pat that Beth seemed intelligent enough, but was causing constant trouble in class. Katie and Pat attempted to tackle this problem in many ways, but the problems continued. Emma was by contrast an amicable, good-natured student, but she too struggled with her schoolwork.

Pat, the children's father, had also struggled to read and write at school, but he was terrific with people and figures and together the couple's business continued to grow.

Months later, Katie became desperate and took Beth in to Cardiff to see a child psychologist. Ranges of tests were conducted and the results were astonishing. Beth was at the highest possible end of the scale for intelligence. The psychologist told Katie that based on her results, Beth was highly gifted. Further testing showed she was also severely dyslexic. Katie said to the psychologist, "What can we do about the dyslexia and how can it be treated?" The psychologist looked at her without emotion and said, "There is no cure. She will be fine. Just go home and get on with it." Katie knew that everything was not going to be fine and unless she did something, things would only continue to get worse.

Katie was relieved Beth was so intelligent. She had suspected all along that she was a smart cookie as she was so verbally bright, quick witted and humorous and also capable of causing incredible mayhem, when she took it upon herself. Katie was, however, devastated by the doctor's comments regarding dyslexia. It seemed that there was no cure and no solution. Just more years of heartbreak, frustration and struggle to look forward to and Emma seemed to be exhibiting the same learning problems as well.

Katie began to understand the reasons for Beth's defiant behaviour. Here was a highly intelligent girl who struggled to learn or operate within a formal school environment because she was dyslexic. Now Katie was left to figure out a solution.

Being a fairly private family woman, from a family where personal weaknesses were not readily talked about, Katie kept the diagnosis to herself. Nobody really knew what dyslexia was back then anyway. Feeling like there was no alternative available at the end of Grade 4, she decided to take her children out of the public school system and home school them. This proved a challenging but rewarding task for Katie and she slowly developed the skills to teach her girls successfully. They all enjoyed the open classroom environment and loved the regular excursions to museums, gymnastics, trampolining and factories.

In their later high school years, both children were ready to re-enter the education system and were sent to a good local school. Katie chose a school which offered a fantastic range of educational and extracurricular experiences, including visual arts, drama, sport, camps and outdoor education, all areas in which her children were capable and excelled. The children continued to struggle with some aspects of their schoolwork, but were highly confident and managed to pass a majority of subjects each year.

The most important feature of this school for Katie was the excellent standard of the teachers. They offered her children versatile and broad ranging teaching methods and the teachers seemed competent and motivated to assist their students to strive to do their best. Beth's behaviour was still challenging from time to time, but both children graduated from high school with a majority pass rate.

Beth is now a highly successful businesswoman and is involved in the development and overseas manufacturing of homeware products. Since leaving school, she has never looked back. Emma travelled extensively and finally returned home to achieve a Diploma of Nursing. She is now happily working at the Royal Children's Hospital in London and travels home regularly to see her mum and dad.

Katie tells me it was never an option for her to tell her girls what many saw as a weakness. She felt that home-schooling was her only option because there was no school help or assistance available to her back then. Today, her children still do not know they have dyslexia. It seems irrelevant now, Katie said. Both are hardworking and highly successful in their chosen fields of work. She does wonder though, what the next generation will bring.

Parents Know Their Children Better Than Anyone Else

As parents and carers it is our responsibility to always try to do our best by our children. An accurate diagnosis of a learning disability is an opportunity to do just that.

This is the beginning of your journey. Use this book as a resource to help you to learn how to help and support your dyslexic child throughout their school years and beyond. Become educated and be specific.

> "As parents and primary carers of our children, we know them best. We know what motivates them, what scares them, what inspires them and most importantly how to show them love and respect. The issue of whether we tell our child they are dyslexic or not, is not as critical as what we do about it."

Understanding dyslexia and how it affects your child will take about as much commitment and time as studying one subject at school. It is achievable, even if you struggle with dyslexia yourself. There are some amazing people and resources available to help you; you just have to know where to look. You cannot rely solely on your child's school to provide an effective education for your dyslexic child. They are, in nearly all cases, not capable of providing all that is required. Use this book to get started. You will be well rewarded. Your efforts will result in a much happier, confident, capable child and with your unwavering support you will have the privilege of discovering how successful your dyslexic child can be.

Three additional eBooks titled - 'How to teach your child to Read', 'How to teach your child to Spell and Write' and 'How to teach your child to do Math', are available for free from the website DyslexiaDaily.com.

Chapter 9

Shouldn't my child's teacher be able to tell me that my child is struggling to learn and may require testing for dyslexia?

There are three factors to consider when answering this question and we need to address them all.

1. Shouldn't my child's teacher be able to tell me that my child is struggling to learn?

Yes! I believe that teachers should be able to inform parents in a timely fashion when their children are struggling to learn at school.

2. Shouldn't my child's teacher be able to tell me that they may require testing for dyslexia?

No! Based on current teacher training and the number of factors that can be impacting on children today, general classroom teachers in most states and territories are currently not trained or qualified to determine why a child is struggling to learn.

3. Should all school children have access to specialists or teachers that are trained to diagnosis learning disabilities in the future?

Yes! Every school should have access to a trained teacher or a specialist with the appropriate training to screen children for learning disabilities in their first year of formal schooling. A number of effective and proven screening tests already exist and are in use in certain schools, states and territories around the world. These tests have been proven to accurately indicate a child's readiness for reading and determine specific areas of strengths and weaknesses.

When I was conducting research to write this book, many parents from around the world told me stories about their sad and frustrated children who were either struggling to learn or had given up trying to learn altogether. Some of these children were six years old, but some were fourteen and had given up on school altogether. I do not believe that this is an acceptable state of affairs based on what current research tells us about dyslexia, how to effectively screen for it and what can be done to support children with it.

Now we need to consider why this is happening and what can be done about it.

DyslexiaDaily.com

> **"It is extremely detrimental for children with dyslexia to experience failure with learning for longer than is necessary. By today's standards it is possible to reliably identify boys and girls at risk of dyslexia before they fall behind."**

Are Our Teachers Effective?

In every English speaking country around the world and at every tertiary institution that provides teaching degree courses, students who are studying to teach 'English', must pass the Language Arts components of their courses in order to receive their teaching degree. To my knowledge this has not changed throughout the history of obtaining a certificate to teach.

Not only must tertiary students who plan to teach English learn how to teach the language, they must also master the skills that go with it, such as reading, writing, spelling, grammar and punctuation. You would also expect that during their teacher training they would be trained to recognise a struggling learner and how to assess the ongoing progress of all of their future students. But can your child's teacher do this? Only you can be the judge based on your personal experience.

Teacher Training In Language Arts

If a teacher cannot accurately assess the learning progress of their students, and write accurate school reports, are they 100% effective? Are they fully accountable to the children they teach, the school they work in, the education system within their state or country and the parents who pay their taxes and therefore the salaries of the teachers? Perhaps not!

In my opinion I believe all of our children's teachers should be held accountable. They should be able to tell us when our children are struggling to learn within an appropriate time frame so we can take action to assist our children before they are exposed to frustration and failure for prolonged periods of time.

Unfortunately there seems to be many children in this situation. Perhaps your child is one of them and maybe you were too. So why does this continue to happen?

We all know teachers are, on the whole, dedicated and conscientious. So are the teachers at fault or does the problem lie in the teacher training courses, ongoing teacher training and our education system as we know it?

"Recent figures from the National Inquiry into the Teaching of Literacy show that half the 34 Bachelor of Education teacher training courses in Australia devoted less than 5% of their four-year curriculum to teaching reading."

Max Coltheart, Director of Cognitive Science at Macquarie University and President of Learning Difficulties Australia

For many Australians this is a worrying statistic which may lead us to question the quality of many of the teaching courses within our tertiary institutions, historically and currently. I do wonder if the statistics are similar in other English speaking countries?

It is a wonderful skill to have the ability to teach English, but just as important to know how to identify and refer children who are not learning at the appropriate rate to specialists who can offer ongoing support. This is one of the main areas in which I believe many tertiary teaching institutions and the education system in general are letting our children down. All teachers must be provided with an ongoing comprehensive education in Language Arts and the associated learning disabilities in order to ensure children who struggle to learn are not left to do so for longer than is necessary.

Competent reading, writing and spelling skills continue to be an integral part of our daily life. These are necessary basic skills, which enable us to operate effectively within modern society. Our governments, education systems and tertiary teaching institutions must be able to train all of our teachers to teach these skills effectively and efficiently to all children.

I believe therefore that a process must be put in place to enable classroom teachers in every school to recognise a child who may be struggling to learn for legitimate reasons. A subsequent specialist teacher should then be available to carry out further diagnostic testing within the school system to determine the exact cause of their difficulty.

How To Identify Children At Risk

It makes sense to me to screen all schools starters for learning disabilities. Dr Sally Shaywitz, Professor of Paediatrics at the Yale University School of Medicine, Connecticut, USA proposes that this should be done when children are entering their second semester of formal schooling at approximately five and a half or even six years of age. At this time they have generally had some exposure to basic sound and letter symbol relationships.

Children's ability to decode words to learn to read using phonological skills follows a natural, logical sequence. This makes it relatively easy to recognise when a child is experiencing difficulty and in which area this difficulty is occurring. There are a number of proven tests which enable specialists to do this. With early diagnosis and intervention, young children can be offered the appropriate support before they begin to fall behind.

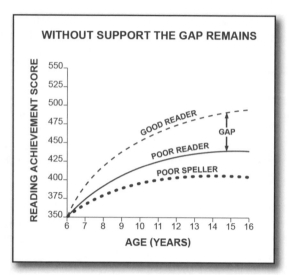

Why We Need To Lobby For Educational Change

The education systems that most of us rely upon are not catering to children at risk of learning disabilities. Many children with legitimate learning disabilities are continuing to fall through the cracks and are being left to struggle through the school years on their own. This leaves parents full of fear and worry for the future with no solutions forthcoming. This is a situation that I believe is not difficult to rectify. Those in power should take note of the readily accessible and current dyslexia research and put an action plan in place to screen children as they begin formal schooling. I believe the funding required for this would be considerably less than dealing with the long term effects of raising future generations of children with reading disabilities, who experience many difficulties and challenges as they move through school and reach adulthood.

Screening Tests To Identify A Learning Disability

There are two types of tests to identify children at risk of a learning disability; standardised tests that all children can take and tests that an individual child can take if specific areas of concern are identified.

In some states and territories, pre-school teachers carry out testing of all the children (4-5 years old) in their care to assess readiness for formal schooling. These tests are generally broad in nature and fairly quick to administer. One of the purposes of these tests is to highlight children who may have a specific learning disability and then offer their parents the opportunity to have more specific testing carried out.

These tests do tend to over-identify children at risk because children at pre-school have such a broad range of skills and life experiences. Some have never picked up a book before, while others can already read. Irrespective of this if parents and teachers have access to these results an appropriate support system could be offered to children in need from early on.

There is no doubt that if all children were screened for learning disabilities as they commenced formal schooling, much of the angst associated with learning at school could be resolved and the learning outcomes and future for so many struggling students could be positive rather than negative. This is not a new concept, there are already schools in countries around the world doing this successfully and a proven track record of success already exists.

Parents who are seeking the introduction of such screening tests into their education system need to find a way to communicate their desires to those in power that make the decisions about educational funding.

Many of us have watched children with a learning disability struggle through formal schooling and know it is not a pleasant experience for the child concerned, or their parents. This should not be occurring. In many countries where such early childhood screening is already in place, it has often been due to active parents coming together as one more powerful voice and lobbying for change.

If all this knowledge exists, why can't teachers tell us our child has a learning disability? Why are so many children being left to struggle without diagnosis or support?

By current standards, most classroom teachers are not trained or qualified to inform us 'why' our children are struggling to learn. In fact many of them would never attempt to do so because they realise they are not qualified and are concerned about any subsequent backlash. There are many reasons why children struggle to learn. It might be a learning difficulty or a learning disability or something completely unrelated.

> **"Imagine if your child's teacher told you that they though your child was mentally retarded or had a behavioural problem like attention deficit disorder (ADD) or was most likely autistic. If inaccurate, you would feel upset, annoyed and angry. This information coming from your child's teacher could also create unnecessary fear and anxiety in parents and their children. More importantly it may or may not be accurate."**

Teacher Opinion Versus Fact

A teacher may believe they know the reason for your child's struggle and may give you their opinion, but that is all it is, an opinion. When speaking with your child's teacher, you should request to see actual examples of your child's schoolwork and class test results demonstrating concrete evidence of your child's actual difficulties. Don't accept anything less. Teacher hearsay and opinion is not helpful when your child is struggling.

> **"Once you have been alerted to an ongoing learning difficulty at school, I recommend you take immediate action to determine the reasons this is occurring."**

Parents Need To Be On The Ball And Follow Their Intuition

Every school is different and all teachers are individuals, as are their students. Because of this it is easy to understand that there are many factors at play every day when our children are at school. It seems that the only way to ensure that our children's educational needs are being met is by paying close attention to what is occurring in our children's schools.

There are some incredibly knowledgeable teachers and specialists working in our schools with years of experience. Listen carefully to what they say, but remember to keep an open mind. General classroom teachers are only qualified to a point, based on their teacher training and experience. Learning support teachers also vary in their range of understanding. It pays to check on the qualifications of your child's learning support teachers. Many learning support teachers have no more qualifications than general classroom teachers.

You can check on relevant qualifications by contacting the dyslexia association within your state or territory, or by asking the teachers directly what specific training they have had for their role. Find out what their qualifications allow them to assess for. They are given the job of providing support to our struggling learners, but not all are appropriately qualified to give you diagnostic information, yet may attempt to do so. Don't allow them to delay your response to your struggling child. You need facts, not opinions. This has happened to me before when I was made to feel that seeking a diagnosis was not required, when it most obviously was. I was made to feel as though I was over-reacting, but the diagnostic tests showed otherwise. I am forever grateful that I stuck to my guns and followed my intuition.

Reasons Why A Child May Be Failing To Learn

It is important when considering the following list how long you believe your child has been struggling to learn. Obviously children will go through different stages throughout their life, so having an intimate understanding of them as individuals and how they function will help you as parents to understand in which direction you should seek help. One or more of these learning, behavioural or emotional problem areas can affect your child:

- A learning disability - including dyslexia
- Attention-deficit/hyperactivity disorders and other disruptive behaviours
- Autistic spectrum patterns
- Anxiety and traumatic reactions
- Mood and emotional problems - including depression
- Environmental and family limitations

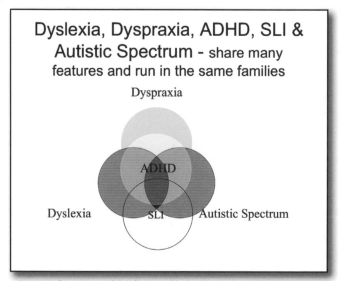

Image Courtesy of Prof. John Stein, Dyslexia Research Trust

Often, caring and supportive parents know or have a suspicion about why their child is struggling to learn at school. Always follow your intuition, but keep in mind there are many of reasons why a child can fail to learn at any age. Becoming educated is your best option to ensure your child receives the appropriate levels of support.

The Many Factors That Affect Teacher Effectiveness

These days teaching children is an extremely demanding and challenging job. There are many factors which can influence the effectiveness of your child's teacher. These are not excuses for poor or ineffective teaching or for not keeping you informed when your child is beginning to struggle, but it is important for parents to be aware of them.

Once a new teacher leaves their place of tertiary study and starts work as a qualified teacher, they invariably enter a very historic institution, that of the education system. As a new teacher, they will be employed by their first school and will walk into their very own classroom for the first time. It is a momentous and exciting occasion for any teacher. In my experience, I don't think years of studying to become a teacher can ever prepare you for the day you walk into your very own classroom for the very first time and face 20-30 expectant faces.

Whether teachers can operate at their full potential is determined by many factors, regardless of how experienced or conscientious they are. Here are some factors to consider, regarding your child's past current and future teachers. These factors can directly influence how effective your teacher is and how successful your child may be at school:

- The personality and skills of the teacher
- How many years of classroom teaching experience they have had
- Any past life and professional experiences or qualifications they bring to their teaching role
- Whether they are parents or not
- The quality of the teaching course that the teacher has completed
- The educational guidelines and standards set by the Educational Department that the teacher operates within
- The leadership, management and communication skills of the Headmaster

- The support systems available to the teacher within the school

- The curriculum - this is a document that states what subject areas and content will be taught, covered and assessed for each year level. Teachers must have a copy of the curriculum and must use it as a basis for all classroom teaching they do. Parents can ask to see a copy of the curriculum at their child's school. The curriculum can also be a valuable resource research tool if parents or carers are seeking to create a tutoring program to support their child or considering a change of school

- The level of experience and expertise of the school's curriculum co-ordinator

- How actively the school's curriculum coordinator monitors classroom teachers to ensure they are following the curriculum, teaching effectively and ensuring students are achieving year level standards

- What levels of ongoing education the teachers are expected to undertake, by way of professional development and educational courses as specified by the school

- The government funding available to the school for the purchase of resources, equipment or to pay the salaries of specialist teachers

- The quality of the teachers that the class has had in previous years

- The students themselves and if there are any pre-existing social, emotional, behavioural and educational factors

- The parents of the students and how supportive they are of school teachers and the educational process

- How the daily timetable is structured and how much time is spent on the direct teaching of each subject

- How many interruptions a classroom teacher and students have on a daily basis, breaking the flow of teaching and therefore interrupting the student's learning

- Noise levels and light in and around a classroom when a teacher is teaching

- The way grade levels are set. Does the school promote straight grade level classes or do they prefer composite classes, which mix the age and grade levels in the same classroom? Composite classes can put teachers under considerably greater pressure as they must teach a broader age group and often juggle two or even three grade level curricula. Composite classes can disadvantage the struggling learner and advantage the highly able student. They can be socially beneficial to many students

- How many times per week individual children leave the classroom for specialist lessons such as music, sport, art, etc.

- The school's discipline policy

- Whether the school has a learning support program and whether that program is ongoing as students move through the school

- The quality of the school's learning support program and the educational background of the learning support teacher/s

- How a school identifies and assists children who need learning support

- How many children are accepted into the learning support program, based on the schools criteria and resources

- The policy of the school in relation to using and training parent and grandparent volunteers to assist students who require learning support

- Whether a school has a policy in place to inform parents that their child has fallen behind based on age appropriate testing and recommend a professional assessment for a possible learning disability

- The quality of the school's testing, assessment and report writing process

- Whether a program of ongoing yearly student assessment is in place, providing a history of a child's learning strengths and weaknesses. This can then provide vital clues to your child's incoming teacher documenting any ongoing struggle or gaps in learning and how the new teacher can assist them effectively

127

- If the school has a professional referral system in place for children whose needs cannot be met or fulfilled by the school
- Whether an effective school committee exists and is a positive influence on the overall running of the school
- Whether an effective parent committee is in place supporting the teachers and children within the school

Children's Strategies To Hide A Learning Disability

Your child's teacher generally spends only one school year with your child. They often see the symptoms of your child's learning disability, not the cause. Remember that children can be incredibly good at disguising a learning disability.

They do this in order to fit in, be accepted and in an attempt to keep up with their classmates, while keeping their parents happy. It is generally not their intention to mislead their teachers or parents, however children develop ways to survive in the classroom and this may lead them to develop strategies to cover up their learning problems. A conscientious teacher may pick up on this, but many may not.

A time will come when finally a child's schoolwork becomes too difficult or an assessment or test result indicates a problem. Teachers may then choose to bring this to the attention of the child's parents, but often months can pass before parents learn the full extent of a child's struggle in class. For a full list of strategies that children may employ to hide learning disabilities, refer to Chapter 15.

Why Do Children Behave Badly?

You only have to read the newspapers and listen to the television news to realise that in today's modern society, children of all ages are dealing with many challenges. We often read and hear about children behaving badly. Why does this happen? Who is to blame? Is it bad parenting, economic pressure, the breakdown of the family unit, poor educational standards, undiagnosed learning disabilities, the media, social networking or technology? Sometimes we forget to consider the origins of these angry, antisocial, violent and manipulative displays of behaviour. It is important for parents to realise that teachers are often on the receiving end of this behaviour and this can make the job of teaching effectively, extremely challenging. It is not hard to understand why teachers often voice their dissatisfaction with their chosen profession or vote with their feet and leave teaching to pursue a new career.

A Note From The Author

I have taught a classroom of eight and nine year olds where at least a quarter of the children in my class came to school each day without breakfast, clean clothes or enough sleep. I had major discipline problems in that class from day one and they put me through my paces, leaving me exhausted. On the other hand, in this class I also had great kids from caring families, who were keen to please, did what was asked of them, worked hard and made good academic progress. It was a real mix, but on certain days the process of actual teaching seemed irrelevant as we organised food, a caring word and a soft place for some of the children to catch up on sleep.

Quite a few of the children in my classroom had social and emotional problems caused by a history of poor or ineffective parenting. Many of the children in my class had minimal support at home from their parents and I don't think schoolwork or hearing their children read at night time, was a major priority for many of the parents. Not all were uncaring, but some were single parents, working two or three jobs sometimes at night to survive and put food on the table. I became one of the only stable and predictable things in many of those childrens' lives.

You know, that was my first job out of teachers college and I still think about those children regularly. Regardless of the adversity many of them faced, they were great kids. I grew to care deeply about them, even Billy, an eight year old boy who caused a classroom riot in my first week of teaching, because I had asked him what his dad did for a job as part of a social studies task. Unbeknown to me, his dad was in jail for attempted murder and aggravated assault. Chairs were thrown, tables were upended and 26 children were all screaming, some in fear and some in anger. It took three male teachers to regain control of my class and I went into severe shock. That was my initiation into teaching. There was no preparation for that at teachers college. That day, as I drove home sobbing, I seriously questioned my career choice of teaching. I felt like a failure. I had let those children down and I had failed to protect them.

I was 23 years old and with the unwavering support of my family, I returned the following Monday morning and began a process which taught me to become a much better teacher. I learnt how to discipline the children, how to show them I cared and how to teach them. In fact, think those children taught me as much as taught them.

Back then, I didn't really understand learning disabilities or whether they were possibly impacting on my students or not, it was more about surviving the day.

The moral of the story is this. As teachers and bystanders, it is very easy to observe other people's children and make assumptions about why a particular child may be struggling at school. Every family is different and children in some families are often dealing with extremely difficult situations at home. Some problems are obvious, others, as we can imagine, are kept well hidden. Teachers are required to support and protect these children, often filling in as a psychologist, pseudo parent, life skills coach, and a watchdog to report at risk children to authorities. While all of this is going on, teachers are also expected to effectively teach children and speaking from experience, I know this can be a challenge in itself. Parents need to be aware of the sort of challenges teachers can face. Many teachers are doing their best to teach and support their students. They should be able to tell us when our children are struggling to learn, but not why, because the reasons can be far reaching and complicated.

Let us assume if you are reading this book you are already in the category of being a supportive, caring and proactive parent. If so, you have a very fortunate child.

Why Your Child Needs You To Arrange A Professional Diagnosis

Until standard diagnostic screening for learning disabilities is in place within schools in your state or territory, it will remain necessary for parents to take action and seek a formal diagnosis for their struggling learner. This is critical to your child's future success, so I recommend you do it as quickly as you can.

> **"It is important to remember that our children do not start school with the intention to fail. Failing to learn is invariably a symptom of something far deeper than just a lack of motivation or laziness. Don't guess, jump to conclusions or take on the opinions of unqualified, well-meaning people. This is not helpful to your child."**

Teachers are invariably dedicated people who teach for the love of the job. Many will tell you it's certainly not for the money. Their heart is usually in the right place. We can all remember the 'standout' teachers when we went to school. These exceptional people are often instrumental in shaping our future and by believing in us they help many of us realise our dreams. Most though, are currently unable to provide you with a diagnosis of your child's learning disability based on their training and experience. This situation is not likely to change in the near future unless we lobby those in power to change our education system to put an action plan in place to do so. Until then, parents will need to become educated to take action on behalf of their struggling child.

Chapter 10

Why school is difficult for so many dyslexic children

What Is The Concept Of 'One Size Fits All' Schooling?

When our five to six year old children start school, have you ever considered the process? We send them off to attend their first day with the belief that the local school is the right and only place for them and that the timing is right. We never question the system, because let's face it, our education system has always been structured the same way, the way we remember it from when we went to school.

Have you ever really thought about how the system works? All the children are thrown in together, taught together and assessed together until they reach their final years of secondary school. The highest year level they successfully complete and the scores they achieve will determine what job they can apply for or which university or college they will get accepted into.

This system is a 'one size fits all' model of schooling, regardless of our individual child's learning differences or their emotional or physical maturity. As parents, we rely solely on this 'one size fits all' system to compare our children's academic abilities and intelligence to all other children. We use this system to guide us, because, for many of us, it is all we know and therefore we never question it.

When we buy a 'one size fits all' garment, it rarely fits all of us. If we are petite it looks like we're wearing a big garbage bag, if we are larger, a corset. Our current education system tends to rely heavily on reading and writing. So if your child is dyslexic the current standard system is probably not going to fit them well.

It is also important to scrutinise the system by which our children are assessed and compared to other children. If you look in detail, you will notice that the system we use to test our children and determine their school success is again a 'one size fits all' model. At no other time in our lives as an entire age group of people are we subjected to these forms of mass assessments and compared to each other, except perhaps when we sit the exam to go for our driving licence and we can choose when we do that. Can you imagine every thirty year old adult having to sit exams at the end of every year to determine what their future will hold?

"So should the child fit the school or should the school fit the child?"

Many school assessments and exams are in 'read the question then write the answer' formats that often create difficulties and disadvantages for dyslexic students. Yet this is often the only option available to your child. So from day one it seems the odds are stacked against your dyslexic child from being able to demonstrate their full potential in a formal school environment. Keep in mind here that dyslexic children are generally of equal or greater intelligence to non-dyslexic children.

By bringing these points to your attention, I do not seek to suggest that schools are going out of their way to fail our dyslexic children, merely to give you and understanding of how a system that has been in place for generations has its limitations for your dyslexic child.

What Is The Education Conveyor Belt?

It is very convenient for parents if a child begins school at approximately five years of age, finishes school at the age of around seventeen, gets a great job or goes straight onto college or university and from there into their chosen field or career. It is the aim of most parents, educators and the government for this to happen and yes, it does make life and paying the bills much more efficient. It is the way the education system is designed and if your dyslexic child can experience success in this way, full credit to them, you and your child's teachers. This is definitely the fast track, but it doesn't have to be the only path to success.

There is no rule that says a child must stay at the same school(s) indefinitely while they complete their primary and secondary schooling, then choose what they want to become when they grow up, in a record time of thirteen years. The world is changing. More and more parents and students are seeing the benefits of changing to more appropriate schools, or leaving school early to go out and experience the world, returning to study at a later time in the life when the student has found their true calling. As parents, don't get caught up in the conveyor belt of the school education system and assume that this is the only way for your child to become educated and to reach their full potential in life.

Look around you. If you think about it, you will be able to identify many people who got onto the education system conveyor belt and have completed long academic degrees, only to discover that they have chosen the wrong path and changed direction abruptly. We can also find people who left school early to begin employment in non-academic roles and then as they developed they became passionate about a chosen career path and achieved incredible tertiary results later on in life. Sometimes people do this via further academic study or via sheer common sense and hard work.

As conscientious parents, it can cause us a lot of anxiety when we consider the thought that our child may be better off changing schools or leaving school early to work. What happens if they never go on to do anything worthwhile? You know your child best and this is a decision you must make as a family. My advice though is never to assume there is only one pathway to achieve success in life. Life is a journey and schooling is a very small part of it.

How To Handle Your Child's School Report

Parents often use their child's school report to measure their success as parents, without realising that their dyslexic child may find it difficult to demonstrate their full potential within the confines of the current school education system.

Zach's story

Zach is a friend of mine and he was telling me his concerns over his son and daughter's school reports. His son struggled across all subject areas and his daughter was a disaster at maths. They had never been diagnosed with a learning disability, but Zach told me they had always struggled at school. Zach's solution was to offer them a large monetary incentive if they could achieve an 'A' in any subject area on their end of year report. I asked Zach if he thought this was a possibility. He looked at me and frowned. "It's probably not very likely," he said, "But I don't know how to motivate them to work harder. What else can I do?"

I even hear stories of secondary school students who are offered cars by their parents if they do well in their final year exams.

> **"When I was at secondary school, I vividly remember a straight 'A' student feeling so pressured by her parents to maintain her high grades and with the added stress of boyfriend dramas, she had a nervous breakdown three months before the end of the year and never sat her final exams."**

We put so much emphasis on our children's school reports. All parents do it. Even I'm guilty of this. It seems they are our only definitive measuring tools. We all stand around chatting and comparing grades, feeling ashamed and responsible when our children do not do well. It's as if our child's school report is a direct reflection on our parenting skills. No parent is guilt free, yet the education system has its limitations. It seems to disadvantage certain children and it has for as long as history can remember. Dyslexic children are operating in a system which currently does not fully recognise their learning style or allow for it.

Keep this in mind next time you receive your child's school report. Perspective is a great thing to have, so don't lose it and let your child think they have disappointed you or let you down. The day your child started school they never set out to struggle and fail or to let you down, only to achieve personal success and to make you proud. These school reports we receive are generally not an accurate indication of our child's intelligence or a predictor of how successful they will be in life and they never will be, unless the system changes and identifies, recognises and celebrates different learning styles.

Fabulous School Failures

If you were to study all the incredibly wealthy entrepreneurs in the world, there is a common thread that connects many of them. Do you know what it is? Many had difficulty at school, failed to learn and many did not complete secondary schooling or failed subjects if they did. When researching this book, I read one study that said that this was true for approximately 33% of the world's entrepreneurs. I have no idea if this is accurate or not, but it's an interesting thought. How do people who performed so badly at school become so successful? Their stories are varied and inspirational.

> **"People with potential will always find a way, even when the school education system does not allow for their style of intelligence. The 'one size fits all' education system in which our dyslexic children operate is not suitable for everyone and it does not determine the true potential of every child."**

> **"I was one of the 'puzzle children' myself - a dyslexic... and I still have a hard time reading today. Accept the fact that you have problem. Refuse to feel sorry for yourself. You have a challenge: never quit!"**

> *Nelson Rockerfeller*
> *Former Vice President of the United States*

DyslexiaDaily.com

"I don't know if I have a learning disability or not, but I repeatedly failed English at school. How ironic that I now make my living as a very successful copywriter, making more money than I could ever have imagined. It wasn't my schooling that did it, that's for sure... living life and having a go taught me how to be successful."

Bret Thompson
Advertising Copywriter

"I was, on the whole, considerably discouraged by my school days. It was not pleasant to feel oneself so completely outclassed and left behind at the beginning of the race."

Winston Churchill
Former Prime Minister of England

"I barely made it through school. I read real slow. But I like to find things that nobody else has found, like a dinosaur egg that has an embryo inside. Well, there are 36 of them in the world and I found 35."

Dr. John R. Horner
American Palaeontologist

"I never read in school. I got really bad grades—D's and F's and C's in some classes, and A's and B's in other classes. In the second week of the 11th grade I just quit. When I was in school, it was really difficult. Almost everything I learned, I had to learn by listening. My report cards always said that I was not living up to my potential."

Cher
Singer/Actor

You can find more fabulous quotes to inspire your children and students on the website www.dyslexiadaily.com.

The education system we have is the system we must use, unless we choose to home school our children or pay for a private school. There is a growing trend to home school, and many success stories as a result of it. It is incredibly admirable if a parent can home school their children and the results are often inspiring. It takes a huge commitment from parents and not all of us have this ability or would choose this option for many varied, personal reasons. Parents also need to be aware that there are also schools becoming available that provide learning and teaching programs specifically for dyslexic children.

Now we have had a chance to consider our child's schooling, how do we support our dyslexic children through the education system as we know it?

Chapter 11

How can I help my child with dyslexia and make their life easier at school?

> **"Life is a journey and schooling is a very small part of it."**

Why You Need To Take The Time To Meet With Your Child's Teachers Before Every School Year Commences

You do this for a number of reasons:

1. To lower your protective parent anxiety levels.

2. To help your child feel less anxious about beginning the school year.

3. To develop a rapport with the teachers from day one, which is important as teachers become a critical part of your support team. It is imperative that they understand what being dyslexic means for your child.

4. To ensure they understand the intricacies of your child's disability.

At the meeting, give the teacher any examples or copies of your child's past work, relevant school reports or specialist reports you may have. Provide them with a short summary of your child's strengths and weaknesses in point form; don't forget to include the psychological aspects. Give them an indication of your child's favourite methods of learning. Add the names of any of your child's classmates who are helpful and supportive of your child and their needs.

In your conversation, include any learning or teaching support structures that your child is used to, or may have found helpful in the past. This may include support teachers, alternative formats, extra time, etc. It is often the case that the parent is the only communication link between a child's year level teachers.

Make sure you also speak with any other specialist teachers who will come into contact with your child. It only takes one small comment or incident to shatter your child's confidence and ruin their day or week.

This simple meeting alone can mean the difference between your child having a happy school year and working to the best of their ability as opposed to having a disastrous year.

"When researching this book I spoke to many teachers. Many said they were often told a child in their class had a learning disability, but not what this meant or how to provide individualised assistance to this child."

Your child's teacher needs you as much as you need them. Don't assume that because they are a qualified teacher they understand your child's disability or what your child's individual needs are. An educated parent invariably becomes the expert.

Why You Need To Stay In Touch With The Learning Support Teacher

At least twice a year, make an appointment to see your child's learning support teacher. Your child may have been having regular contact with this teacher via individual or small group lessons. Find out what your child has been doing in these sessions and what progress they are making.

Learning support teachers are often responsible for conducting an annual school based educational assessment on all students at certain age levels. If this is the case, you can ask them to explain the results to you in detail. These results can pinpoint what learning gain your child has made in terms of years and months, based on their chronological age. You can also look at the average gain of the students in your child's class and compare your child to the average.

If this is not a standard assessment at your school, ask your learning support teacher if they are qualified to provide you with this information. It can provide a good general indicator of how your child is progressing. Many children with learning disabilities will be operating at a considerably lower level than their peers, so focus on their rate of progress as opposed to comparing them to non-dyslexic children.

Developing a good relationship with your child's learning support teacher can also be mutually beneficial for your dyslexic child. If your child is having a particularly rough day, the learning support teacher is often a good person for your child to confide in. They will often have great teaching and learning aids that you can borrow to use at home.

Take the time to discuss with them who they would consider to be the best teacher for your child the following year and why. You can be sure that learning support specialists know exactly who has the right set of skills to help your child. Once you have been given some options, speak to the school Headmaster well before the school year ends to try to have your child allocated to this teacher's class.

Be aware though, that this may mean separating them from their supportive friend network. I would think very carefully about moving them away from their friends, especially in the older grade levels when friends become very important.

Sometimes, knowing who the most appropriate teachers are for your child can point you in the right direction if you decide to go down the path of using one as an after school tutor. Schools will have varying policies on this practice.

Why It Is Critical To Use Email To Stay In Touch With Your Child's Teachers

Endeavour to stay in constant contact with your child's teacher. Staying in regular personal contact is beneficial, but not always easy, so email can be fast, effective and efficient.

Email works both ways and to everyone's benefit. In the busy world we live in, it is a great instant communication tool.

You can keep the teacher informed as to what is affecting your child on any given day, for example;

- When your child is tired/sick
- When something has occurred to make your child anxious or stressed
- When they are struggling with a particular school project or homework task
- To ask if a learning exercise can be modified to better suit your child
- When there is an opportunity to celebrate a personal achievement and reinforce positive self-esteem
- When you would like the teacher to help you to achieve a particular goal
- To ask their advice
- To tell them about a new strategy you are employing at home to help your child

The teacher can also keep you informed:

- When assessments are coming up. This means you can arrange extra practise if required and help to mentally prepare your child, or it can allow you the opportunity to review the test format and ensure special allowances be made to suit your child
- When you child has had a particularly challenging day and needs some extra T.L.C. (Tender Loving Care)
- If your child is having difficulty with a task, so you can assist at home
- To let you know if an activity can be modified to better suit your child's needs.

An Example Of An Email To A Teacher

Dear Mrs P

I wanted to ask you when you would be changing the seating structure in your classroom again. Ellie is enjoying school, but finds her current position, towards the back of the desks with her back to the whiteboard, difficult. I had her eyes tested last year and she

has perfect 20/20 vision. She is however, coming home mentally exhausted. I know she struggles with the visual concentration required for classroom school work and last night curled up in my lap and asked me if I could speak to you about moving her closer to the front.

I am working hard with her at home to help her to keep up with her classmates and increase her automatic reading rates, using the flash cards you provided me. I believe there has been a little jump in her literacy skills just recently and her confidence is increasing.

Let me know if is possible to move her. I would appreciate your feedback.

Kind Regards,

Glenda Patterson

How To Repair A Communication Breakdown Between Parents, Teachers And School

When our child is constantly struggling at school and they are beginning to exhibit signs of emotional stress, we as parents can also become distressed. No one likes to see their child in pain, whether emotionally or physically. Having a child with a learning disability can cause emotions to run high, as we want the problems to be rectified. We want solutions to be found and the pain our child is feeling to go away as quickly as possible. In many cases, parents wait too long before they go into the classroom to raise an issue, which is causing distress, making them ripe for an altercation with a classroom teacher.

Teachers are often on the receiving end of our angst as we seek to understand and find answers to our questions and concerns. It is not difficult to become frustrated by the school system when we are seeking change in the lives of our struggling children and none seems to be forthcoming. So what can we do when the relationship between parents and teachers sours and our children are suffering as a result?

"I am a great believer in communication and this is often the best way to overcome a soured parent teacher relationship. A communication breakdown is to our detriment and more importantly to that of our struggling child. They will be the biggest loser in this scenario."

Here are four options to consider, depending on your situation:

1. Find a teacher, specialist or parent who can mediate on your behalf. You can explain your child's situation to this individual and ask that they assist you to rectify the communication breakdown to help you to find solutions for your struggling child within the school system.

2. Wait until the end of the year when you can get a new teacher, start fresh and move on. This can take time though and your child needs constant ongoing support.

3. Change schools because you are not getting anywhere with the school hierarchy.

4. Repair the damaged relationship between yourself and your child's teacher and move forward together in an effort to support your dyslexic child.

You have the right to advocate on behalf of your child and choose any path you wish, but if you choose to try to repair the damaged relationship here is one suggestion.

The Apology Approach

Make an appointment to speak to your child's teacher. During the meeting, apologise to the teacher for your handling of the situation to date. Explain to them the reason for your tone and your choice of words when you speak to them. You need to reiterate that this is a direct result of the worry and fear you feel for your struggling child.

You might be thinking 'Is she mad? There's no way I'm going to lower myself and apologise to that hopeless teacher'. An apology, although hard to give, is a great way to wipe the slate clean, get teacher's back on your side and move forward as a team once again. Explain to the teacher that you just want some reassurance that your child is receiving the best opportunity possible to operate at their full potential.

Everyone can relate to feelings of despair and worry. Being humble often takes courage, but this is a strategy that can work to get parent/teacher communication back on track. Teachers will often become more sympathetic to your plight and more pro-active on your child's behalf.

Dealing With A Problem Teacher

At some time you will most likely encounter a teacher or a school Headmaster who is inflexible, uneducated and unwilling to make concessions for your child. This often comes down to their personality, their style of teaching or leadership and the classroom standards they enforce. These teachers can be very intolerant, hostile and verbally abusive towards your struggling child. If your child's self-confidence is taking a battering, you need to take action fast. You can tackle this scenario in a number of ways:

1. Seek to educate the teacher. Build them up by making them feel like they are the dyslexia experts. Do this by providing them with educational material and strategies and then asking for their feedback.

2. Use another teacher from within the school with a proven track record of effectively teaching children with learning disabilities to speak to this teacher and advocate on your child's behalf.

3. If you have the time, volunteer in your child's classroom to get a sense of what is occurring.

4. Ask the school Headmaster to intervene.

5. Ask other parents if they have witnessed any verbal abuse or mistreatment of your child – document and date their responses if relevant. It is more powerful to have proof when you are seeking a solution from authorities.

6. If all these strategies fail, get your child away from this teacher as fast as possible. Arrange counselling if necessary and start considering your options whether this means changing schools, contacting educational authorities or seeking legal advice.

Why It Is Important To Keep A Logbook For Your Child?

From the moment you suspect that you child is not learning at the same rate as others and may have a problem, it is very important to keep a record of your observations. If you have a work diary, you can use that, or if you prefer keep a notebook handy. When appropriate, jot notes into it. Make sure you always include the date.

There are a number of reasons for this. Firstly, it is often hard to be objective about our own children, so writing down our observations can help us to clarify our thoughts. Secondly, this logbook will become a resource you can refer to when you are seeking assistance for your child.

> "I would recommend a special notebook. Date and record every contact; personal, phone or email. Make a note of who said what and what outcomes were agreed. Keep copies of every note and letters sent and received. Accurate records can become a powerful negotiating tool."
>
> *Margaret Hardy, Dyslexia Testing*
> *Services Australia*

You should include:

- Any specific difficulties with learning you might observe. For example: 'Tyler keeps complaining of headaches when reading his reader', or 'Eliza keeps misreading small words of two letters – sometimes missing them altogether'.

- Keep a record of any meetings you have with your child's teachers. Include who was present, what was discussed and what the outcome was.

- Include any specialist appointments you have. These could include specialists from within the school or in the wider community. Again, make a note of who was present, what was discussed and what the outcome was.

- Make notes of any support strategies you are using or any educational programs that are being offered to your child. Include when they started, what is involved, how long the program runs for and how they are being measured. It is also a good idea to make a note of what your child thought of the program.

- Keep a record of any verbal reference your child makes to being treated badly by students or teaching staff. At the same time, always include references to positive school experiences your child has in relation to particular students, teachers or school events.

Keep a file for your child of any documentation that is being generated in relation to your child's education. This can include letters, reports, contact lists, etc.

Why An Accurate Diagnosis Is Critical To The Support Your Child Will Receive At School

Get your child formally diagnosed. Having a formal diagnosis of your child's learning disability is a must if you want to ensure your child has access to all the educational considerations that are available to them. As parents, this is an important part of ensuring your child is provided with the best possible opportunity to succeed within the school system.

DyslexiaDaily.com

A diagnostic report can be an important tool for parents because it establishes that your child has a diagnosed learning disability. If you have had unhelpful teachers and Headmasters in the past, this factual document cannot be ignored and requests instant action be taken on behalf of your child to assist them.

A formal diagnosis can, depending on your school and the state in which your child attends school, allow for remediation, modification and accommodation.

A Remediation

A remediation refers directly to a learning program that caters to your child's identified areas of weakness. This invariably means your child may leave class to have access to a learning support teacher and a program that is intensive, direct, multisensory and systematic. It is worth asking whether the programs your school uses are evidence based or scientifically proven, as some states in certain countries have a prerequisite for this to be the case.

A Modification

A modification refers to changes made to the year level curriculum to cater for your child, such as:

- Rewriting grade level expectations
- Reducing the number of curriculum expectations to be mastered
- Writing alternative expectations for your child
- Selecting expectations from a different grade level

"Curriculum modifications are not always appropriate. It is better to try and maintain grade level expectations and modify the environment or the response mode so that children can complete work at their intellectual level."

Dr. Paul Whiting – Sydney, Australia

An Accommodation

An accommodation refers to any assistance that enables your child to access the grade appropriate curriculum. These can vary considerably but may include:

- The use of teaching methods deemed more appropriate for your child
- Extra personalised assistance in the school classroom
- The extra provision of time to complete certain projects, tests and exams
- The option for your child to sit tests and exams in an alternative area. This can mean they feel less pressured during exams. They may be placed in a room where there is less noise and minimal distraction
- The provision of a teacher's aide to read questions for your child on certain tests and exams
- The provision of a scribe to write answers for your child in certain tests and exams
- The option for your child to read aloud the written questions on tests
- Not being penalised and having marks deducted for spelling errors when spelling is not the focus of the evaluation
- Access to recorded audio text books
- Complete oral assessments
- Use of electronic spellers
- Using a laptop to complete classroom work instead of writing
- Recording lessons so they can listen to them again at a later date
- Access to a peer note taker
- Changes to the font size, paper colour and amount of text per page on written tests
- Use of voice recognition software for writing and print to speech software for reading text

Use this information to find out and secure the education considerations for your dyslexic child. This may be in the form of a Learning Support Plan or similar document, which is created specifically for your child and sets out what the school is putting in place to support your child. It is important that parents are involved in this process to ensure a complete understanding of what is being organised to help your child and how it will be evaluated.

Legal Protection For Your Child With Dyslexia

Every state of every English speaking country in the world has a different set of legal standards for dyslexic students, as described in the Chapter 3. It pays to be aware of your legal rights.

> **"In Australia there is no legal right to assessment, but once a child is assessed and diagnosed with dyslexia, then the Anti-Discrimination Act protects children's rights through the Disability Standards for Education 2005. All educational institutions in Australia must provide appropriate support for students diagnosed with a disability including dyslexia."**
>
> Margaret Hardy, *Dyslexia Testing*
> *Services Australia*

In other countries where the law is not so definitive dyslexic assessments can still be obtained, but this is not always a legal right.

You can find out more information on this topic by searching on the internet for your particular area's Department of Education and then go to the 'special education' link. There should be information for you to access online. There are also lawyers who specialise in representing children with learning disabilities.

Be aware if you decide to take legal action against your educational authority, win your case and are awarded damages and a monetary payout is forthcoming. The payment is often taken out of the state's education budget.

Please be aware legal action can be time consuming and expensive, which may take your valuable time and resources away from supporting your child.

15 Strategies To Ensure Your Child With Dyslexia Has A Good Day At School

1. Ensure your child consistently gets a good night's sleep. Children with dyslexia often have difficulty operating at their full potential when they are tired.

2. Make sure they eat a healthy substantial breakfast. This will put fuel in their tank and give them energy to learn. On this same note, make sure you provide them with a healthy lunch and dinner as well, including some whole foods. If you allow them to eat high sugar, high fat, over processed junk food, expect their brain capacity, concentration and behaviour to be rubbishy too.

3. Make sure they have a good supply of fresh, cool water to drink throughout the day. This keeps the blood supply flowing to their hard working brain. Many schools are happy for students to take insulated refillable water bottles into the classroom these days.

4. Create a standard weekly schedule for school and afterschool activities. Include on this schedule which uniform your child is expected to wear on a certain day, a list of all items that need to go in their school bag each day and pencil in any additional activities that need to be taken into consideration.

5. Provide them with a monthly wall calendar so they can plan tasks ahead to ensure they allow plenty of time to research, work in stages, and take their time. You may also like to provide them with a yearly planner to allow them to keep track of tasks and time on a larger scale.

6. Encourage them to utilise the best time of the day to practise their reading or complete their homework. Some children with dyslexia work much better in the mornings than the afternoons and evenings.

7. If homework is taking longer than is suggested for your child's year level, it is important to contact your child's teacher. Children with dyslexia should not be spending hours struggling with homework after school. It pays to keep teachers informed if this is occurring.

8. Write a note to remind you of any additional communication that needs to occur that day between yourself and a particular teacher or specialist. For example: Email Mr B about Rebecca's exam accommodations.

9. Give your child access to a computer and a typing tutor program. Word processing can be a major bonus for many dyslexic children. The earlier they learn the better.

10. Help your child to organise their personal space and belongings and then encourage them to keep them organised. This may mean having a place to store all the items that need to go backwards and forwards to school throughout the week. Perhaps there could be a series of coloured plastic paper trays for school tasks that need to be completed today, this week, this month or this term. Provide them with access to a desk in a quiet part of the house where they can complete their homework.

11. For middle and senior school students, it can be helpful to hire a second set of school text books – one set for home and one set for school. Many school textbooks are also available in electronic formats, which can be a useful tool for your child.

12. Be available to support your child when school tasks become overwhelming. It only takes a few minutes to help your child to clarify their thoughts and put a process in place to give them the confidence to tackle a school task. Take into account a timeline to complete the task to ensure it remains achievable for them.

13. Monitor the amount of television they watch and computer games they play. There have been hundreds of research studies on this, but to keep it simple I call the TV the brain draining, grumpy box. In my household it seems to drain my children of productive mental energy, while causing a major decline in attitude and behaviour. You may need to do some research on this in your household. If you decide to wean them off electronic media, I can warn you it will take about three weeks before they stop asking for it. Replace it with all kinds of before and after school activities. These can include cooking, swimming, sport, charity work, playing at friend's houses, building cubby houses, gardening, visiting grandparents, etc. My children are not allowed to access electronic media (unless educational) between Monday and Thursday. Find the compromise that suits your children best. Too much TV causes brain drain in my opinion. Remember, don't just exclude your child with dyslexia; it must be one rule for all to be fair.

14. According to Dr. Alexandra Richardson, it is very important to provide your child with enough Omega 3 fatty acids every day. The best source is oily fish such as herring, mackerel or salmon. Dr. Alexandra Richardson is one of the UK's leading authorities on the impact of nutrition and environment on the brain. Through her research she has brought hope and help to 1000's of children with learning disabilities. Much research indicates that both Omega 3 and Omega 6 fatty acids are vital nutritional supplements, as they cannot be made within the human body, yet they are critical to cellular structure and optimal brain performance. Omega 6 fatty acids tend to be in excess in modern diets, but few people eat enough oily fish, so the correct Omega 3's (EPA & DHA) tend to be in short supply. Her research studies indicates that supplements of these fatty acids can promote improvements in behaviour, increases in concentration levels and better learning outcomes for children with learning disabilities, among many other benefits. Experts recommend 500mg of EPA and DHA (long chain highly unsaturated fatty acids – LC H.U.F.A.s). Omega 3, specifically EPA and DHA, is readily available in the form of fish oil capsules. Make sure you check the contents and amounts

on the label as many fish oil tablets do not provide what is recommended. Please refer to Dr Alexandra Richardson's book, 'They Are What You Feed Them' for more important information on this topic.

15. Always keep communications lines open on a daily basis. Your child with dyslexia needs to know that no matter how busy family life gets you are always available to talk to them.

Let Your Child's Teacher Know What Your Child Needs In A Teacher

If you were to ask your dyslexic child for an instruction manual to create the perfect teacher, what would it include? It seems that some teachers are easy to learn from and others are not. The South Cumbria Dyslexia Association, UK and the Manchester Metropolitan University (MMU), UK, surveyed dyslexic pupils about how teachers made learning - easy or difficult. Some of the dyslexic pupils' comments are listed below. Why not use this information to ask your child's teachers if they could put some of these practices in place to assist your dyslexic child?

- At the start of the lesson, be clear about what you want us to do
- Don't give too many instructions too fast
- Show us how to do something as well as tell us. Use pictures and structural material – these make it easier to understand
- Be prepared to repeat the instructions
- Teach the basic information – 'without rambling on about other things'
- Show enthusiasm for the subject
- Let us ask questions – check that we are doing it right
- Proactively check we are doing it right
- Smile when we ask for help – explain it again and do at least two examples with us
- Write things neatly and clearly – preferably on a white board
- Leave instructions/spellings etc. on the board for a long time

- Help us when we get stuck
- Be patient with our mistakes and when we need help
- Be nice to us – please do not shout when we get it wrong
- Number lines at both ends – different coloured lines can also be helpful
- Prepare notes to minimise copying from the board
- Put homework instructions in audio formats or on the school website
- Accept and encourage work to be presented in different forms – audio, web cam, oral responses etc. 'You choose the best way to show me what you know for this task'
- Create a peaceful environment in the class

"Never lose heart and never give up. Parents and teachers are often the critical point of difference in the life of a dyslexic child."

Chapter 12

How to decide if your child should repeat a year or change schools

To Repeat Or Not To Repeat?

Also known as grade retention, this is where it is suggested that your child repeats a year in order to catch up academically. There are positive and negatives arguments for and against this practice. Here are a few things to consider if you are thinking of having your child repeat a school year, or if a school suggests this to you:

- The chronological age of your child
- The level of maturity of your child
- Their social skills, networks and friends
- The numbers of school days missed due to illness or absenteeism in a particular year
- The psychological impact on your child
- Ask yourself - Will the positive benefits far outweigh the negative benefits?
- Ask yourself and your child's school - How will repeating directly benefit my child?
- Ask yourself and your child's school - What processes will be put in place to assist my child in the coming year?

Repeating your child or retaining them is something you need to consider very carefully. Children with dyslexia do not outgrow it or become instantly cured as they mature. You know your child best; so don't allow others to make this decision for you and your child.

> **"You must make this decision for yourself because as a parent you will be responsible for the long-term ramifications of it."**

There is a huge social stigma attached to repeating a school year. Children are well aware of it, and schoolyard talk can have a negative impact and follow your child throughout their school years. Students with learning disabilities do not generally benefit from repeating a year. In some instances an academic gain due to repeating can be attributed to covering the same year level content twice, yet research indicates the psychological damage caused by repetition can far outweigh this benefit.

You also need to keep in mind that your child cannot keep on repeating. Children with dyslexia generally need ongoing educational support, not just more of the same. They do not need the message that you do not believe in them and feel they are unable to keep up with their peers. Maintaining their self-confidence is more important than a report card when it comes to being successful in life.

As you can see, I'm not generally a fan of repeating children with dyslexia, but there are times when repeating your child may be more appropriate for example.

Times When It May Be More Appropriate To Repeat

> When your child is changing schools altogether

> If by repeating them you are placing them at a more appropriate chronological and/or social age

> Your child becomes eligible for educational services that are not available if they move up a grade

> Your child would have access to a teacher with particular skills to benefit your child

> Your child is requesting it; make sure you discuss their fears and concerns in depth

> Your child is changing schools and the new grade level curriculum is more challenging

> If you are moving inter-state or inter-country and schools have different age and educational standards

> You have decided to delay entry into middle school or high school in order to offer them a school or home school catch up year.

When teaching, I had cases where younger children who were not psychologically or socially ready for school were held back and repeated their first year of formal schooling. This can be highly beneficial because academically and psychologically they can go from the bottom of the class to the top of the class instantly the following year. Many young children I observed gained enormous confidence from this experience and maintained it for years to come.

The opposite can occur if you retain children based purely on academic ability and disregard intellect, maturity, friends and social networks. They feel left behind and often they stay left behind. In my mind the ability to get along well with people is more important than academic skills. We all know how important networking is.

> **"Remember the old saying – it's not what you know, it's who you know".**

In most cases, your child is operating in a formal academic system, which creates educational limitations for them. If it is your belief that your child is of equal or greater intelligence to those around them, do not insult their intelligence by making them repeat a year unless appropriate.

How To Choose The Right School For Your Child

The choice of school for most parents comes down to cost and convenience. Even if you do not have the luxury of choosing a specialised school for your child with dyslexia, you may have the opportunity to choose one school over another within the suburb or region that you live.

> **"No two schools are ever the same, so never make this assumption. People run schools and people are all different."**

Choosing your child's school can be one of the most important decisions you will ever make, so do some research and put some thought into it. You are not trying to find the perfect school, because it doesn't exist, you are trying to find the perfect match of school for your child. If you get the school right, it can mean the difference between happiness and success for your child or ongoing struggle and failure.

How To Find Out If A School Is The Right One For Your Child

The best way to research a prospective school is to ask questions. These are some of the people you should seek out to speak to:

- Parents whose children already attend the school
- Parents of children who are identified as having a learning disability who attend the school
- Education specialists, dyslexic assessors and child psychologists who work in the area surrounding the school
- Teachers and teacher aides at the school
- Learning support teachers from within the school
- Police officers from within the local community policing squad

39 Questions To Ask A School Headmaster When You Are Choosing A School For Your Child Or Considering A Change To A New One

Once you are well researched, the final person you should speak to is the school Headmaster. Questions you might like to ask are:

1. How many students attend this school?
2. What is the average class size? Does this vary throughout the age groups?
3. Do you offer composite, (mixed age classes) or straight age levels?
4. What is the ratio of male to female students?
5. What is the ratio of male to female teachers?

6. What is the average age of the teachers?

7. Do they have teacher assistants in the lower grades of the school?

8. How many teachers are qualified or trained as learning support teachers?

9. What is the preferred teaching approach utilised by this school: formal, informal, practical, theme based, multi-sensory or other?

10. Can you give me some insight into the school's preferred method of teaching reading, spelling, writing and math? Ask which programs the school uses. You can quite often research their effectiveness via the internet.

11. Are there any additional features or programs being offered in this school that I should know about?

12. What subjects do children leave the classroom for, e.g. music, sport, spelling, art?

13. How many teachers/students have left the school in the last three years? You can often tell if a school is having difficulties through teacher and students turnover in the last three years. If numbers seem higher than you would expect, ask them why they think this is the case?

14. How many student free days do you have per year in addition to school holidays?

15. What is the school's expectation for the ongoing professional development of teachers and learning support teachers?

16. Can I have a copy of the school curriculum?

17. Does the school offer a broad curriculum that will support your child's strengths? A quick note here - highly academic schools can prove challenging for children with dyslexia, but many of these schools also offer excellent, music, performing arts, science, hospitality, graphic design, engineering, information technology, sport and outdoor education programs. These are all areas in which children with dyslexia can excel. This can be a

plus if it allows your child to explore their strengths and build their self-esteem. You will need to weigh this up.

18. What does the school excursion and camp program include for each year level?

19. What is the school's behaviour management or discipline policy? Ask about their policy for bullying and anti-social behaviour too.

20. Do they offer pastoral care, a school counsellor or a psychologist?

21. How many children with learning disabilities does the school have? Ask for specific numbers of children with dyslexia.

22. What is the ratio of qualified learning support teachers per number of students who require extra support?

23. How is special education or learning support provided for children at particular class levels? Do they leave the classroom and receive instruction individually or in small groups? How many times per week does this occur? How long are the sessions?

24. Which educational programs is the school currently using in the learning support program? Make a note of these so you can do further research. Ask how successful the programs are. You can also ask how they measure their effectiveness and also whether they are evidence based.

25. What resources and equipment are available to support children with learning disabilities?

26. How often do teachers in the special education department liaise with other teachers and specialists within the school who come into contact with your child?

27. What is the school policy on providing remediation, modification and accommodation for your child during normal class work and during tests and exams?

28. What are the strengths of this school? Are there any areas in which the school is trying to improve?

29. What are the homework expectations for each year level?

30. Do they offer any extension programs for highly gifted and talented children? You may also like to check if the prerequisite for access to a 'gifted program' is high academic grades or whether children with high-level intelligence who do not do well in formal testing are also included.

31. How does the school keep parents informed about how their children are progressing? What does the school reporting program entail? Are students assessed purely on academic ability or is student effort included?

32. How are computers utilised within the school?

33. What is the school's preferred method of communication between parents and teachers?

34. What is the schools policy on parental involvement?

35. If you were to choose this school what does the orientation program involve?

36. Can you see a school canteen or tuckshop list?

37. Are foreign languages compulsory?

38. Do they stream by class and subject? If so, at what year level does this occur? Streaming is grouping students based on their academic results and capabilities to be taught different levels of the same subject. For example, some students may qualify to do basic math as opposed to others who may qualify to do more advanced math subjects.

39. If parents were going to complain about something – what would it be?

One More Thing.....When You Visit A School, Consider The Following

1. What is the overall environment like? – I call this 'the vibe'

2. Do the children seem happy and content?

3. Are staff members receptive to you? Are they happy to answer your questions and do others respond warmly as you come into contact with them within the school?

4. Is there a sense of order, unity, teamwork and productivity?

5. Observe classes in session. Note how the classrooms are set up, what is displayed on the walls, how the children are behaving, interacting with others and responding to teachers and your presence.

6. Follow your intuition and gut feeling as to the character of the school and what it can offer your child.

Chapter 13

I've heard about coloured glasses.
How can I tell if they may
help my child?

Reading Glasses Versus Tinted Lenses

As soon as you see someone wearing reading glasses you assume that they have a problem with their eyesight and need glasses to see accurately. We wear sunglasses to reduce glare and protect our eyes from harsh sunlight. As we get older, we may notice a preference for choosing sunglasses with particular coloured lenses. I prefer peach coloured sunglasses; my husband Andrew prefers dark blue/grey. By choosing a peach colour, I am meeting the needs of my eyes. I find the colour soothing, I see the world in richer more defined colours and my eyes feel more rested and recharged.

So how can coloured glasses help our children? Often the first thing we do when our children begin to struggle to learn at school is to get sight and hearing tests done to ensure that poor eyesight or hearing is not the cause. If this possibility is ruled out, sometimes we are left confused as to what factors are affecting our child's success at school. So why can tinted lenses help children with learning disabilities even when their eyes seem to be working perfectly?

Tinted glasses have been around since the 1980's as a method for assisting people with learning disabilities to read, but up until recently much speculation and controversy has existed about whether they actually work or not. Medical science is again helping to clarify some of the doubts.

What Are The Meares–Irlen Syndrome And Scotopic Sensitivity?

New Zealand teacher Olive Meares was the first to document spatial distortions of text, while pupils were reading in a remedial clinic in 1972. She also noted that the extent of the distortions could be reduced or eliminated by using tinted plastic overlays.

American psychologist Helen Irlen, working in California, documented similar findings. She called it Scotopic Sensitivity Syndrome (SSS) or Irlen Syndrome. In 1983, she presented a research paper to her branch of the American Psychological Association in which she announced her findings. This research paper concluded that text distortions were considerably reduced if coloured filters or overlays were used for reading. Helen Irlen continued her research, publishing reports and developed a protocol for screening for scotopic sensitivity. This included the creation of an assessment system for distributing coloured overlays to those who would benefit.

Professor Wilkins and his colleagues at Essex University, UK, were among the first to use medical science to examine the concept of scotopic sensitivity, and in doing so went on to establish a range of tools for screening for the condition. The screening tests that resulted are available to professionals today and are known as the Intuitive Overlays Test, whilst the tool used to quantify the effects of the overlays is known as the Wilkins Rate of Reading Test.

Ongoing research indicates that a high percentage of visual dyslexics can be assisted through the use of tinted glasses and eye exercises. It is therefore well worth assessing whether your child is a candidate for this type of assistance if they are showing the signs and symptoms of having visual dyslexia.

How Does Scotopic Sensitivity Tie In With Visual Dyslexia - Is It The Same As Having Visual Processing Problems?

Having visual dyslexia can also be described as having visual processing problems or 'perceptual dyslexia', a term favoured by the Irlen Institute. Scotopic sensitivity describes the symptoms of having visual dyslexia. The symptoms may include, amongst others, text described as wobbling or jumping, words running together with no spaces, or seeing only the spaces between words like rivers running down the page, flickering, blurring, text changing size, halo effects, glare or the like. There are many things to consider if you believe your child may be affected by visual dyslexia.

How Does The Eye See?

Our eyes are an incredible piece of biological equipment. Light goes through the windshield (the cornea), through an opening in the iris called the pupil, through the lens and then hits a tissue lining, the inner surface, called the retina, which acts like the film in a camera. The retina then triggers a complex sequence of chemical and electrical nervous responses sent to the brain, which recreates the image. Many experts believe that a person with visual dyslexia experiences difficulty due to the defective timing and chemical processing of the image in the brain.

The Signs And Symptoms Of Visual Dyslexia

Dyslexia is a broad term which often describes a combination of both auditory and visual processing difficulties. It is important to remember that no two dyslexics will ever exhibit exactly the same set of symptoms even when they are from the same family. It is possible to have just visual or auditory dyslexia or a combination of both.

Visual dyslexia refers only to those symptoms which are a direct result of processing problems related to what a person sees.

There are many, many symptoms of visual dyslexia.

Some of these can include;

- **Light Sensitivity -** Sensitivity to certain types of lighting or bright lights such as the sun, car headlights or artificial lighting such as overhead fluorescent lights.

- **Glaring -** Problems with glare from white or glossy surfaces such as white paper or classroom white boards. Glaring can also compete with dark print on a page, making letters, numbers and musical symbols more difficult to see. An Irlen assessor with fifteen years' experience indicated to me that in her experience there is often a common trait shared by those with visual dyslexia; and that is light sensitivity, which can cause the whiteness of the paper to dominate the text. Not only can the white dominate, it can also begin to bleed over the top of text and children can lose the smallest words on the page in a blur, or lose the starts and ending of larger words. Children become unsure when reading and attacking unknown words, whether or not the whole word is actually there. To experience this, pick up a book with a page of text and hold it open flat. Keeping it horizontal, lift it up to your eye level so you are looking across the page. Now the white rivers that exist between the words will become more obvious to you. It is these white rivers that often glare and flicker for visual dyslexics, making it difficult to accurately see the words. In some instances the glaring can be so extreme that it actually distresses a child to look at a page of text or makes them feel ill.

- **Text Movement –** Although text is obviously static on a page, those with visual dyslexia often see varying degrees of text movement when reading. The text may simply move in the same way each time and then stay put in its new position, making it difficult to decipher, or it may continue to move around while a child is trying to read it. See examples further along in this chapter. One of the problems with visual dyslexia is that if a child always sees distorted text they can assume it is normal and never mention it, thinking that everybody else sees it the same way.

  Other children may realise that this is not how the majority of people see words and they start to believe there is something very wrong with them. Using a pointer like a finger or a ruler can often work as a method to help the text behave.

- **Processing Rates –** When our eyes scan a page of text to read, our eyes flick from word to word, from left to right. Each flick is known as a 'saccade' (some specialists refer to this as tracking). The eyes focus (fixate) on each word between saccades for about one third of a second. We only see the word during these brief fixations to gain meaning. Visual dyslexia reduces the efficiency of fixation, making our children much slower than their peers. When a competent non-dyslexic person reads, they automatically recognise a word, or often they only have to look at the first two or three letters to predict what the word is, making their reading fluent and effortless. Those with visual processing problems often need to look at the word for much longer and break it up into word parts in order to decode and understand it. This makes them slow and cumbersome readers. Memorising strings of letter and numbers enables us to chunk groups of letter and number symbols together. Think back to when you copied something down, like a recipe from a magazine or somebody's address. How many numbers and words could you hold in your memory before you begin to write? Many dyslexic children can be limited in this way, only being able to memorise one or two letters in their head before they have to write them down to remain accurate. This can take enormous mental energy. Copying from the chalkboard can be a nightmare for your child. If writing spelling words out five times each is your child's teacher's preferred method of learning new words for the test on Friday, this may be a totally ineffective way to learn spelling words for your child. I think back to my school days when certain children had to write 100 lines for bad behaviour, such as 'I will stop calling out in class and behave'. It makes me shudder as I remember how difficult it was for some children, taking all lunchtime and sometimes after school to finish.

- **Comprehension** – Comprehension is the ability to gain meaning from text, to understand what the text is telling us when we read a story or a non-fiction book. Sometimes when we drive our cars, we don't recall the exact details of how we actually arrived at our destination. The same can happen when reading. We see the words, our eyes move over them, our brain processes them, we think or speak the words aloud, but we do not gain meaning from them and have no idea what we just read. It usually indicates it's time to take a break or close our book at night and go to sleep because our brain is tired. This can be an ongoing feature of visual dyslexia. You may realise this is occurring when you start asking questions at the conclusion of a reading session about what your child has actually read. Another feature of visual dyslexia which can affect comprehension skills is the enormous amount of effort it takes some children to decode individual words in a piece of text. This effort can dominate the reading experience so children may be saying, 'What is that word?' rather than,' What is this story about?'

- **Visual Perception-** How we interpret space and objects around us is probably the easiest way to describe visual perception. Depth of field, dimension, speed of objects moving around us, speed of words and numbers flashing on the computer or TV screen, how we see light and dark and shades in between. Visual dyslexia can affect all of these visual perceptions and as a result many areas of a person's life skills can be affected, such as reading, writing, spelling, maths, copying, reading music, learning new languages, computer skills, driving (particularly at dusk), night vision and sporting performance.

- **Concentration Levels -** Some children seem to be able to sit still and happily read a book or work on a task for hours; others only read or work for a few minutes and then lose focus on the task. Their eyes start darting around the room and they wriggle in their chair. Visual dyslexia can be the reason for this lack of concentration as their brain struggles to take in a constant stream of visual information and focus is lost.

- **Strain and Fatigue –** Many children will start a reading or writing task, happily working away, only to find their eyes and brain begin to tire more quickly than those around them. The outcome of this can be losing concentration, feeling tired and sleepy, eyes that become dry and itchy or sting. Sometimes headaches can result due to ongoing tension and eyestrain. When these children start an activity they can see perfectly, but after a period of time, strain and fatigue can set in causing text to become distorted. At night, when we sit with our children to practice their reading, you will sometimes notice their levels of competency will waver from night to night. It can be baffling and frustrating for parents. Why were they reading so well last night and tonight they can't even correctly attempt a word they are familiar with? In many cases this is a direct result of strain and fatigue. Often when they are struggling, it is better to try again in the morning when they are fresh, take it in turns to read a sentence, read to them instead or use an audio book from your local library.

The Big Secret

Children are smart and after a while they begin to question what they can see. They look at children around them and notice that they do not seem to be experiencing the same things when they are attempting to read.

> **"Maybe they even say to a friend one day, "When you read, do the words ever move around on the page?" and the friends replies. "Don't be silly, of course not."**

This confirms their darkest fear and they begin to assume they are dumb or something is very wrong with them. Time moves on and they continue to struggle until schoolwork becomes more difficult and they just can't seem to keep up any more. The big secret is kept, because no one will believe them anyway and parents and teachers can begin to assume that the child is just not very smart.

It is often during an assessment for visual dyslexia that the floodgates open and years of self-doubt came to the fore. Finally somebody is asking them if the words always stay still or do they play tricks? The child can't quite believe what they are hearing. 'Maybe this person understands; maybe they know what I am going through and they will believe me'. So many years of believing that they are at fault, and something is very wrong with them can take its toll on a young person. The relief they experience is phenomenal, regardless of age.

Proactive Cameron's Story

Cameron was eight years of age and in Grade 2 at school. He had always been a below average reader, but loved stories and worked hard to decode words to gain meaning, practicing regularly. Three students in his class had greater difficulty reading than he and as the causes for this were eventually uncovered - they all started to wear reading glasses.

Cameron started to think, I can see clearly, yet my eyes start to hurt when I copy from the whiteboard. Sometimes the letters go fuzzy and my head hurts. Why do I always mix up the little words? Maybe I need reading glasses too? He went home and told his Mum, Jane. "Mum, I think I need glasses. I am having trouble seeing the whiteboard".

Jane was not convinced about the glasses, as he had had eye tests before and he never exhibited any other signs of poor eyesight. However she took him for an eye test, as things change and it was important to rule this out. The eye test indicated he had perfect 20/20 vision. Cameron was confused, something was not right. What could this be? At his Mum's request, the teacher moved Cameron closer to the front of the classroom and this helped, but did not completely stop the monster headaches he often had after school for no apparent reason. Time wore on and reading still remained difficult, which Cameron found frustrating as he had an amazing imagination and he used books to feed this.

Finally, his Mum decided it was time for some further testing and took him to a learning disability specialist for assessment. As you probably guessed, he had visual dyslexia. Dark blue overlays seemed to assist him enormously. He was not keen on wearing glasses, so plastic overlays were used to assist him while reading. Glasses may be the next step as he matures. He has now gone up two reading levels since his last school reading assessment, Jane happily reports.

Sam's Story

Sam was six and in Grade 1 at school. He was struggling to remember simple words and was making very little progress learning to read. Sam was beginning to exhibit signs of distress. However, his Mum Fiona decided to wait the year out to allow for natural development and to see how he progressed next year. Things did not improve.

Later that year a family holiday to New Zealand meant a huge catch up with all of their friends and family. Sam's struggle to read came up as Fiona chatted to the other Mums about their children. One of the Mums knew about visual dyslexia and strongly recommended that Sam be tested. Fiona was not convinced, as Sam was only six, but she decided it would be an interesting exercise regardless of the outcome. She was in for a shock, as testing indicated that Sam was only seeing the tops of the words and the bottom of the words and in the middle of the words was a long white blurry strip. This of course made reading words extremely difficult, Sam was constantly confusing the letters, even though he was trying hard. A blue overlay was tried during the assessment and Sam sat up in amazement. "All the letters are joined back up again', he said. 'The spaces have gone." Fiona couldn't believe it, she was so happy for Sam. He now has blue glasses and is doing so much better at school. Fiona is forever grateful to her knowledgeable relatives in New Zealand. When I spoke to Fiona five months later, Sam had made amazing progress and was now among the top readers in his class. He was a different boy altogether his mum said, and he now enjoys school immensely.

Sarah's story

Six year old Sarah was struggling to learn to read and as a result she was in learning support at her school, doing reading recovery. Her teacher Michael noticed that Sarah kept her arms and hands protectively around the outside edges of her book. Michael asked her to put her hands back in her lap so she could concentrate fully on her reading. Within moments Sarah had put her arms back again.

"Why do you keep doing that?" Michael asked her. Sarah looked up with a frightened expression on her face.

"If I tell you, will you send me back to pre-school?"

"No! Of course not," said Michael.

"Do you promise?" said Sarah.

"Yes", said Michael.

"If I put my arms there," said Sarah, 'it stops the words from running to the edge and falling off. It keeps them on the page so I can try to read them."

"Oh! I see," said Michael, but he wasn't quite sure what to make of it. It seemed impossible, yet Sarah didn't look like she was making it up.

What Might Your Child See When They Look At The Printed Page?

The following are examples of what your child may see if they are affected by visual dyslexia or visual processing problems.

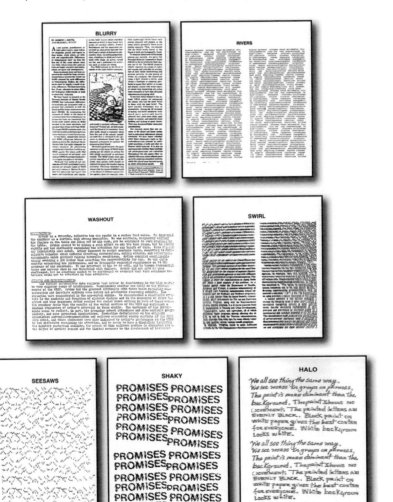

Images Courtesy of Helen Irlen

27 Questions To Ask Your Child If You Suspect They May Have Visual Dyslexia

1. A great question to start with was suggested to me by an assessor at an Irlen Diagnostic Clinic in Melbourne Australia. 'Do the words always play tricks or do they behave?'

2. Does reading make you tired?

3. Do you often lose your place when reading?

4. Do you sometimes skip words when reading?

5. Do you ever re-read the same words over again?

6. Do you skip lines altogether when reading?

7. Do you sometimes read words or numbers back to front? For example; 'was' for 'saw' or '64' for '46'?

8. Do you often misread words when reading? Like 'them' for 'there'?

9. Do you find it easier to keep your place on the page by using a pointer, like your finger or a ruler?

10. Do you find it hard to keep concentrating on the printed page - are you easily distracted?

11. Does the white on the page ever feel too bright or hurt your eyes?

12. Do you become restless and start to fidget?

13. Do your eyes become watery or sore?

14. Do you squint to see when reading?

15. Does it help to close one eye when reading?

16. Do you want to rub your eyes when you read?

17. Do you keep your eyes close to the page when reading?

18. Do you hold the page you are reading further away from your eyes to see clearly?

19. Do you prefer a particular light when you are reading – is it dim or bright?

20. Does the white paper in the books seem to glare, flare or flicker at you?

21. Do you see white rivers running down that page in between the text?

22. Do you ever see white cracks on the page?

23. Does it become harder to read the longer you are reading?

24. Does the text seem to move around or become blurry?

25. Does it seem like there is a spotlight behind the word flickering while you are trying to read?

26. Do you prefer one font size or style to another?

27. Does schoolwork give you headaches?

The next chapter gives possible causes for visual dyslexia and explains how to tackle it.

Chapter 14

So what causes visual
dyslexia and what can be
done about it?

What Is Visual Dyslexia?

Having visual dyslexia is defined as having ongoing sight to brain processing difficulties. The eyes receive the information when we see, the nervous system passes this information to the brain along the optic nerve and the brain then processes this information, for us to access it and make it meaningful.

Professor John Stein has conducted many studies in an attempt to understand what causes visual dyslexia and why coloured lenses help. He uses the Magnocellular Theory to describe his research findings. Magnocells are a system of large neurones which are specialised for timing visual information. When our brain receives visual cues for processing, magnocells are responsible for the rate and accuracy of response to these cues. They rapidly fire, passing information from our eyes to our brain and we respond accordingly.

John Stein's research indicates that the visual magnocellular system directs visual attention and eye movement and is mildly impaired in many (but not all) dyslexics. Some of these impairments include:

- Visual magnocells are about 30% smaller in the dyslexic brain
- A reduced response rate to visual information creates a slower response to visual cues in dyslexics
- The eyes' response rate to moving objects is slower in many dyslexics
- The eyes of dyslexics are prone to wobbling, making it difficult to focus on printed text. Research studies indicate that the more a child's eyes wobble, the worse a child's reading
- The cerebellum - the control centre for body movement, located at the back of the brain, exhibits a reduced response rate
- There is a lower sensitivity to low light levels, movement and depth of field
- Poorer ability to focus, visual attention and slower visual search often exists

- Visual crowding can occur, with objects appearing to bunch together
- The speed and timing of visual information as seen by the right and left eye can differ, as can the processing rate of the sight receptors within the brain. Because we have two eyes, the information received by both needs to come together accurately. This is called 'vergence' and can be likened to the way we see through a pair of binoculars. Research indicates that many dyslexics have very unstable vergence control, meaning the eyes' nervous system is not working in perfect harmony because there are timing differences. It is important to know that this magnocellular system is also very vulnerable to drugs and disease.

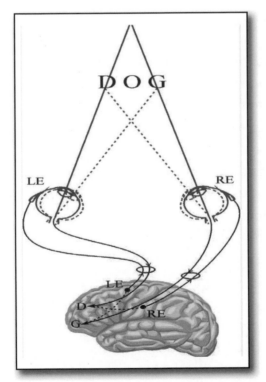

Image Courtesy of Prof. John Stein, Dyslexia Research Trust

19 Things Your Child Might Say When Reading If They Have Visual Dyslexia

Children with visual dyslexia often think that there is something seriously wrong with them. They may need your reassurance and encouragement to reveal what they can actually see. Have faith in them and remember your child never set out to struggle at school. Below are some of the things they may say. Keep in mind there are thousands of variations of these symptoms and they can range from very slight to very severe:

1. 'The letters go all blurry'
2. 'The letters move over each other, so I can't tell which is which'
3. 'The white lines that go across the page cut the words in half'
4. 'The white wiggly lines that go down the page are distracting'
5. 'The lines of words seem to go in waves'
6. 'The letters seem to float all over the page'
7. 'The letters split and go double'
8. 'Letters are shaking like they are shivering'
9. 'The words are spinning'
10. 'The letters move in and out of the page'
11. 'Letters are moving around the page like ants'
12. 'The c moved over the r, so it looks like another c'
13. 'The p joined up with the c'
14. 'd's and b's sort of get the wrong way round'
15. 'Copying work from the board takes forever'
16. 'My page goes all glary and hurts my eyes'
17. 'I keep losing my place on the page'
18. 'Reading gives me a headache'
19. 'Reading makes me tired'

DyslexiaDaily.com

Why Do Coloured Lenses Help?

According to John Stein, when reading, children's difficulty to see, then decode the letter symbols into sounds and then words when reading can be explained just by lower levels of visual magnocellular sensitivity, regardless of a child's intelligence. Therefore, lower levels of visual magnocellular sensitivity interfere with how well a child's reading skills develop.

John Stein's research shows that many children with visual dyslexia show considerable improvement in reading with interventions that improve magnocellular functioning and eye control.

He has scientifically tested three methods to improve the effectiveness of the magnocellular functions:

> Eye exercises to control eye wobble

> Coloured lenses to encourage an improvement in magnocellular performance and hence reading rates

> Patching of the left eye to improve eye vergence or binocular stability.

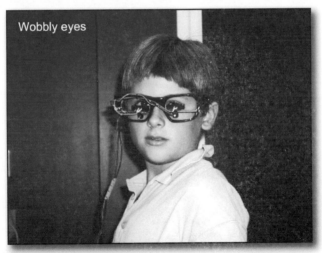

Wobbly eyes

Image Courtesy of Prof. John Stein, Dyslexia Research Trust

Approximately one third of children with visual dyslexia showed significant improvements in reading rates. On average, the children increased their reading age by six months after just three months of treatment. Most children then continued to improve even after treatment was complete.

Coloured lenses are thought to help dyslexic children by rebalancing the input and timing of visual information as it travels from the eyes to the brain for processing via the optic nerve.

Why Do Yellow Lenses Work?

John Stein has determined that the magnocells on the retina of the eye (the layer of cells at the back of the eye that are sensitive to light and trigger nerve impulses that pass, via the optic nerve, to the brain where a visual image is formed), receive visual stimulation from both red and green receptor cells. This makes them very responsive to yellow light. Therefore yellow lenses assist this balance, improving the timing of the visual magnocellular system. This makes the brain more receptive to the visual cues coming from the retinas in both the left and right eyes. The nervous system in both eyes becomes more synchronized. This improves vergence control and binocular vision because the optic nerves for both eyes now work properly together.

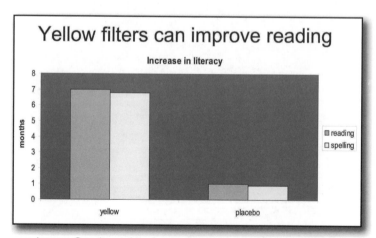

Image Courtesy of Prof. John Stein, Dyslexia Research Trust

Why Do Blue Lenses Work?

Image Courtesy of Prof. John Stein, Dyslexia Research Trust

According to John Stein's research, only 10% of retinal receptor cells respond to blue, indicating they probably have a very small overall input into the visual magnocellular system. Nevertheless, it is thought that blue lenses work by increasing the arousal of the visual magnocellular system. Optic nerve pathways are enhanced and the visual nervous system works more effectively. This can create many benefits for dyslexics. John Stein's research shows that, for many dyslexics, blue lenses make the text behave, stopping it from moving around and becoming distorted. John Stein has noted an even bigger improvement in reading rates for dyslexic children who showed a preference for blue lenses.

Blue glasses have also been documented as a solution to headaches caused by eyestrain and tension. A word of warning though, yellow glasses can make headaches worse for some individuals.

> "By clarifying the role of the visual magnocellular system in reading, it has enabled us to develop techniques to help 75% of the visual dyslexics we see to, on average, quadruple their reading progress."

Professor John Stein

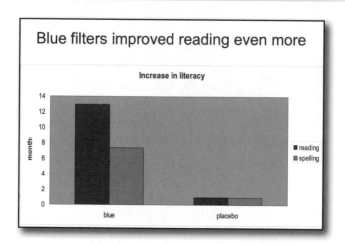

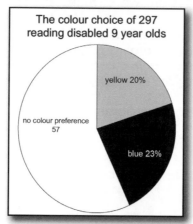

Images Courtesy of Prof. John Stein, Dyslexia Research Trust

Although such interventions obviously do not assist every struggling dyslexic learner, such amazing results can only give hope to the many parents of children who continue to struggle with visual dyslexia and therefore reading.

How Do I Get My Child Tested For Visual Dyslexia?

Accurate testing for scotopic sensitivity can be conducted by the Irlen Institute, which has clinics worldwide. There are other specialists who may give you an indication as to whether your child may be a candidate for tinted lenses; however the Irlen Institute offers extremely comprehensive testing. Irlen recognises that there are approximately fifteen shades of colour to consider and of those colours there are between four to eight tones within each. Blue for example can be an almost non-existent almost clear tone, ranging up to a deep midnight blue. Irlen believes that the exact depth of colour can be critical for your child, which is why proper testing is so important.

John Stein's research indicates that precise colour is not so important in creating a reading improvement. His research indicated that only one shade of deep blue or deep yellow created the best magnocellular response in children who had a preference for either blue or yellow lenses. The tints used are Standard Wratten filters, available from any photo shop or from Oxford University in colours Yellow (negative blue) No 15 and Blue 47b. The Dyslexia Research Trust at Oxford and in Reading in London, UK, also offers an excellent scientifically based service for testing for visual dyslexia.

Dyslexia assessors and optometrists with appropriate training may also be able to provide you with testing to indicate whether your child is a candidate for tinted lenses.

For a comprehensive list of testing centres for visual dyslexia or visual processing difficulites please go to the service provider directory at www.dyslexiadaily.com

How To Introduce Coloured Lenses To Your Child And To The Classroom

By the time a child is struggling with their schoolwork and making limited progress with their reading, their self-esteem and confidence levels are often affected. The thought of introducing coloured glasses which would make them stand out even further as being different can be daunting for both the parent and the struggling child.

Depending on the child, the successful introduction of tinted lenses can depend on how old they are, how confident they are, their family, their teacher and the reaction of the other children in their class. So how can you negotiate around these issues?

Obviously coloured lenses work best when they are worn as often as possible for reading and close work; visual processing does not just impact on reading. If a child finds the benefit of wearing the tinted glasses great they will want to wear them. If their reading rate and the speed at which they can successfully complete their schoolwork improves drastically, then the wearing of the glasses will be directly linked to their new-found and ongoing success. It pays therefore to make a concerted effort to encourage your child to wear coloured lenses if it has been proven via assessment that your child falls into the category of a child who can be assisted via this method.

A self-conscious child who is already feeling different and does not under any circumstances want to appear any more so, is a different case, and often a very hard case at that.

What is important is the use of the coloured tint to assist the efficiency of visual processing system. Here are some strategies you could try.

- Get the tinted glasses made and insist your child wears them for their own benefit. Call a meeting with your child's teachers requesting that the teacher reinforces your preference for your child to wear them whilst at school.

- A method that worked with my son when he was diagnosed with yellow glasses was to have the lenses made up into sunglasses. He didn't want to wear reading glasses, but it was cool to wear sunglasses at school.

DyslexiaDaily.com

- Ask your child's teacher if you could do a presentation in your child's classroom as a way of introducing your child's new coloured glasses. Take a variety of tinted acetates (plastic) into the classroom and let all the children have a play with them while trying to read. If you are good at computers why not make up some reading activities on the computer with different coloured backgrounds ask all the children to raise their hand as to which background colour they prefer. Use the example of sunglasses on a bright day. Talk about the optic nerve and how it works and then explain why your child sees better with tinted glasses and how it will help their schoolwork. You may also like to talk about how common dyslexia is among the English speaking population. Education is often the best way to pre-empt questions and reduce opposition to a new idea.

- Ask your child to wear the glasses only when they are at their desk doing schoolwork or at home doing homework but not at sport or in the playground.

- Have two sets of glasses made, one for home and one for school, so children do not have to remember to transport them from home to school each day. This avoids a well-worn excuse for not having them available at school.

- Instead of using glasses, order sheets of tinted acetate (plastic) in your child's preferred colour to lay over the top of worksheets and school books. This method is not as effective as wearing glasses, but can help none the less. It will be an effective measure to assist reading, but will not assist with writing, which needs to be considered.

- Use a tinted reading ruler.

- Provide the school with a ream of tinted paper in your child's preferred colour and ask the teacher to photocopy all worksheets for your child onto it.

- Ask teachers to be mindful of the photocopy quality of worksheets provided for your child. Poor photocopies are often difficult to read.

Will My Child Always Need Tinted Glasses And Will They Always Have The Same Coloured Tint?

If your child has been diagnosed with visual dyslexia or are indicating signs of visual processing difficulties and tinted glasses have been proven to assist them, then wearing tinted glasses will be an advantage. As schoolwork increases in difficulty and more reading to learn is required, any aid that makes this process easier will be an advantage. The assistance coloured filters can give to a child is often enough for their vision to improve permanently and they won't need the filters long term.

On the other hand, as your child develops and moves through school, their preference for different coloured lenses may also change as their effectiveness alters. Sometimes your child will be the best judge of this and will tell you that their glasses do not seem to work as well as they used to. A yearly assessment is often the best way to keep abreast of this.

My husband Andrew will often put his blue tinted glasses on when his eyes are getting strained and tired from long hours in front of the computer or reading. The boost the glasses gives his eyes enables him to continue working at an appropriate rate to complete his tasks.

Jack's Story

Jack was sick of his tiring job as a builder's labourer, his back was giving out and he had decided it was time to change careers. The problem was he had never been very good at reading. After thinking long and hard about his future prospects he decided to begin a business degree at night school and enrolled in three subjects. Jack was more than capable of completing the course work, but his reading rate was slowing him down. He would often find himself still reading his textbooks at 3am. As he was still working during the day as a builder's labourer he was becoming more and more exhausted.

Finally Jack thought he couldn't keep it up any longer. He was just so tired and his day job was beginning to suffer. He had decided to admit defeat when he heard about testing for visual dyslexia and tinted glasses. Luckily for Jack, blue tinted glasses worked. His eyes were capable of so much more when he was wearing them and his reading rate improved enormously. Jack continued with his business degree and is looking forward to earning his degree next year.

Sally's Story

Sally was first fitted with her tinted lenses when she was nine years old. They were not a magic wand, but they did make words easier to read; the white of the page was not as bright and she could read for longer periods of time without becoming tired. Importantly, her levels of fluency also increased and she started to read with expression. Sally was so much happier and she began to feel good about herself after beginning to feel like she might be dumb and stupid. Sally's mum, Lynne, compared the glasses to a pair of crutches supporting a broken leg; the glasses supported Sally's reading and made it easier.

Sally became worried after about eleven months as her glasses did not seem to be working as well anymore, so she told her Mum. Lynne became concerned and did some research. She discovered that the coloured lenses can have a use by date, because they alter the amount of light going to the retina and therefore alter the timing of the nervous message along the optic nerve. Over time, the brain begins to adjust. In order to continue to be effective the tint needs to be checked via an annual assessment. After the assessment Sally's lenses moved from purple to blue, to paler blue, and then to grey which she maintained through her final year of secondary school as the work load increased.

When Lynne first took Sally for Irlen screening in 1998 she was told up front that the colour of the tint required would probably alter over the years and then once Sally hit puberty her preference for a particular colour would most likely stabilise. 'This is just what seems to have happened', said Lynne. 'I don't understand the exact science behind the lenses, but I know that completing secondary school with her self-esteem intact would have been extremely difficult without them. The glasses helped to make words easier to read. They filtered out refracted light, reduced the contrast on the page and dulled the glare from fluorescent lights. More importantly, they gave Sally hope. They made a difficult task easier and the difference was enough for Sally to believe she could do it – and she did. She started university this year and we are thrilled'.

Chapter 15

The psychological effects of struggling at school

A Day In The Life Of Your Child With Dyslexia

Being dyslexic invariably means your child faces an ongoing struggle to learn and produce schoolwork every day. This can put your child under immense, enormous, horrendous and relentless pressure. Nobody except the struggling child can imagine how this feels day after day, year after year, until his or her plight is recognised, if ever.

As parents who see their children after school each day, this can be observed basically in the context of good days and bad days. On good days, the dyslexic child's struggle will hardly be noticeable as the classroom tasks and subject areas are well within their range of capabilities. On bad days, everything comes tumbling down. Maybe they had a spelling test where the results were made public or maybe they were asked to answer a question or read aloud and other children laughed at them.

After difficult days at school our children will walk in the door under a cloud and sometimes as parents this is the first sign we get that something isn't right. The built up stress and frustration has to go somewhere and it is often taken out on family members, brothers and sisters and more specifically the primary carers, such as mum or dad.

Children, as a general rule, begin school fairly resilient, happy, carefree and eager to learn. They want to be a success. As they start school they are nervous with anticipation at the prospect of being at school with the big kids, excited to be starting their formal education and eager to learn to read, write, do sums and to prove themselves.

Unfortunately for the child with dyslexia, this is where things can start to go horribly wrong. Tasks that seem relatively easy to everybody else are hard and confusing, if not impossible and your child does not understand why. They try harder and harder to complete their school tasks the way everybody else seems to be able to, and yet are completely mystified as to why they are struggling. To add to this burden, parents are often totally unaware of their child's struggle, which can create even greater stress for the child.

As the struggle continues other classmates will begin to notice and make comment. Your child with dyslexia will be upset and confused and not wanting to bring further attention to themselves or to disappoint their teachers or parents, they begin to develop strategies to cover up their difficulties. Alert teachers may notice your child's struggle at this stage and will allow plenty of time for your child to develop.

"This is because children start school with an enormous range of abilities. Some can read, some don't yet know their alphabet, some can count to 100, some can't count to 10, some can tie their shoelaces, some can't find their shoes."

Teachers must allow for these differences and the general rule is that after a couple of years at school all the children will have caught up, unless of course they have a learning disability like dyslexia.

As times marches on and years pass by, school becomes increasingly difficult. As academic standards rise and expectations are higher, your dyslexic child begins to struggle to keep their difficulties hidden. On the inside they begin to doubt themselves and their self-worth and their confidence levels begin to plummet. They begin to think something is very wrong with them, that they are flawed.

This lack of confidence and self-worth can manifest in various ways, depending on your child. This can be coupled with high levels of anxiety as your child tries to keep their struggle hidden and keep up with their classmates.

We all know that feeling we get when we are suffering from anxiety; knots in the stomach, rising panic, light headedness, shaky, sweaty and often an inability to think clearly and act normally. Imagine being able to predict that you will experience this feeling at some point every day. You never know however, when an anxiety attack is going to hit, because you don't know which activity is going to trip you up and reveal your dyslexia, or what the reaction of others will be. It could best be described as living life in a pressure cooker of fear and anxiety, never knowing when the lid is going to blow off and everybody will get to see the contents of your mind and soul.

This constant anxiety can eventually begin to take its toll on your child; it becomes obvious and observable in many varied forms. We can't see the feelings of despair and anxiety, but we can see the symptoms of it.

A List That May Describe Some Of The Symptoms And Outcomes Of Your Child's Struggle To Learn

Displays anger and frustration

> Becomes verbally and physically abusive towards family, teachers, students and others

> Destroys possessions and personal property, including schoolbooks, public property and family possessions due to frustration and anger

> Gets angry with themselves and has meltdowns when they are not coping. May make comments about how dumb and stupid they are

> Becomes easily annoyed and angry with others when things are not going their way

Exhibits disruptive classroom behaviour

> Will create diversions when confronted with a task they feel they cannot achieve successfully and without discovery of their dyslexia

> Becomes a smart aleck to prove they are intelligent, even though they struggle with the written word

> Refuses to do their schoolwork

> Becomes abusive, rude and outspoken in class towards teachers and students to take the focus off their schoolwork

> Asks to go to the toilet or leave the classroom repeatedly to get out of doing schoolwork

> Pretends to be ill so they can spend time in the sick room to get out of doing schoolwork

> Hides to get out of doing schoolwork

> Will not stay at school and leaves the school ground without permission

> Skips school altogether

Experiences times of extreme sadness

> Has times of sadness and despair when they are inconsolable

> Becomes emotionally upset and cries easily for little or no reason

> Has periods of time when they experience melancholy and nothing will cheer them up

> Has occasions when they do not want to leave the house because they are feeling down

Lacks self confidence

> Constantly makes comments that they are hopeless, no good or 'just can't do it'

> Refuses to 'have a go', even when there is a support system in place

> Places little worth on a contribution they have made

> Refuses to attend activities or events because they feel they have nothing to offer

> Will not speak up in class, in conversations or in a social setting, because they feel they have nothing important to say

Suffers from feeling constant embarrassment

> Feels exposed when they are in a situation where they feel people are looking at them always fearing the worst

> Feels inferior to others even when they are seemingly equal

> Avoids or refuses to be the centre of attention

> Won't answer questions or make comments, even when they know the answers or have something to contribute

> Tries to avoid being seen or bringing attention to themselves

> Is lonely and refuses to mix socially or have friends because they feel that they don't fit in or can't keep up academically with the other children

Feels exhausted and drained

> Comes home after a day at school mentally exhausted and drained

> Struggles or refuses to do homework because they are too tired

> Avoids practicing reading because they are too tired and would prefer to be on their computer, watch TV or sleep

Withdraws

> Stops taking part in classroom activities

> Refuses to do their schoolwork

> Prefers to spend time alone

> Will complete their schoolwork to the best of their ability, but does not speak or respond unless spoken to directly

> Goes through the motions of physically being present, but is not mentally engaged in what is going on around them

Are feeling bullied by life in general, the system, teachers and/or other students

> Comments that they hate school

> Feels as though the whole world is against them

> Complains constantly about teachers, students and school and how mistreated they are

> Has difficulty fitting in and finding friends

> Will sometimes comment that they have had enough and that they want their life to end
> Can be verbally bullied by teachers and physically and emotionally bullied by students who have no understanding of what it means to be dyslexic
> Becomes a bully because they constantly feel bullied

Experiences anxiety and panic attacks

> Is nervous to the point of being unable to think clearly or act appropriately
> Even when capable of a task, their anxiety levels are so high they are unable to perform it
> They feel sick to the point of physical or mental illness
> Will bite nails, grind teeth, pull out hair or cause themselves physical harm

Experiences depression

> Clinical depression is more than just feeling sad or having the blues. It is more a sense of helplessness and hopelessness over a prolonged period of time. The ramifications of depression can be serious and ongoing. Children who struggle with dyslexia are thought to be in the high-risk category for developing depression. This is not something you can or should try as a parent to manage by yourself. I urge you to seek professional help if you feel that clinical depression may be affecting your child with dyslexia.

Why Parents Are So Important When Their Children Are Struggling

So now we are beginning to understand how our children might be feeling and how they may personally react to the challenge of being dyslexic. More importantly, it is time to develop some strategies to help them to increase their emotional strength, build their self-esteem and reinstate their self-confidence. We can assist them to do this by helping our children to change the way they feel about themselves. By building self-confidence, we provide a tool that can lead our children on a journey to personal success, triumph and happiness.

> **"Research is showing that children who are resilient and learn how to manage their dyslexia have better long term outcomes."**
>
> *Margaret Hardy, Dyslexia Testing Services Australia*

Why Earlier Assistance Is Better

It becomes apparent at this stage why it is so important to recognise and diagnose your child's learning struggle at the earliest possible time, whether they have dyslexia or another learning disability.

Not only can you assist your child through the learning process, you have an opportunity to help your child to build a solid foundation of self-worth and value.

If your child has struggled with dyslexia for years before diagnosis and support has been provided, it may take more time to help them to feel good about themselves. It is important for you and your child to know that there is a light at the end of the tunnel. There are plenty of examples of amazing dyslexic people who have remained undiagnosed for years and have gone on to become incredibly confident and successful people.

How We Cope With Life Directly Impacts On Our Children

We all know what happens when we have a bad day and are feeling out of sorts and cranky. Before we know it, the whole family is driving us crazy and the situation seems to go from bad to worse. Without realising it, we have created a grumpy household and it continues to spiral out of control until we realise what has happened and put a stop to it, or another factor intervenes and changes the course of the day.

Children feed off our moods, our stress and our fears. Imagine that in your family you are the sun and your children are the planets orbiting around you. Whether you realise it or not, you often set the tone in your household. Your happiness is therefore a critical factor in the happiness of your children.

Because of this close family relationship, the way we react to our child's learning disability can also have a compounding effect on our children. In fact, I think you will find that there is a direct relationship between how parents cope with the adversity of a learning disability and how their children learn to as well.

This doesn't mean we can never let our family know we are having a bad day or experience a melt down every now and again. That's life, and it is important that our children see us going through everyday trials and tribulations, then recovering and getting on with it. We teach them more about coping strategies than we realise in this way.

Emotional problems like stress, anxiety, anger and depression tend to become more exaggerated in our children when they are constantly exposed to more downs than ups in their everyday lives. Children need to operate in a mainly positive environment in order to develop healthy coping skills and natural resilience.

Often the best way to learn to do this is by becoming educated and talking to others in the same situation that can offer you support and hope. You need to be able to imagine and foresee the potential of your child and the successful future that awaits them.

"Remember the way you felt when you suspected or discovered that your child was dyslexic? If your reaction was a negative one, you need to remember that your child will not learn to cope with being dyslexic until you come to terms with the fact that you have a child with dyslexia."

If you choose to see a counsellor or a psychologist to assist you or your child with this process of overcoming your fears and concerns, you need to be congratulated for being proactive. Try to ensure that you choose one who has an understanding of dyslexia and learning disabilities. You wouldn't go to a heart specialist to treat an eye infection. The same rules apply to counsellors and psychologists.

Chapter 16

How to put a support system in place for your child with dyslexia

Teaching Your Child To Seek Help When Necessary And Getting A Support System In Place

A dyslexic child can never feel confident without a support system in place. They need to feel as though they can ask for help whenever they require it.

A good support system is critical to your child because it can help your child to:

- Feel confident enough to be able to operate at their full potential and to do their best at school
- Have the confidence to try new things and 'have a go'
- Have the confidence to meet and mix with new people
- Have the confidence to strive to reach their goals
- Have the emotional strength and confidence to overcome obstacles and adversity.

The most important people in this support system are you and your family.

You will also need to recruit your child's school teachers, learning support specialists, school friends, classmates, extended family and family friends.

Use all you know about your child with dyslexia to educate the members of your child's support group. The word 'dyslexia' means different things to different people, so keep your explanation simple. It is important to be specific, so that they understand when their help may be required. You may also need to be specific in describing the ways in which your child may need help and support. The people in your support team may have a tendency to complete tasks for your child, rather than providing the support which enables the child to do the task for themselves. There will be days when your child feels so challenged that they will need a helping hand to complete a task, but it is important to remind them we are not teaching learned helplessness, but providing support so they can complete a task confidently by themselves. Remember to tell everyone that having dyslexia is not an indication of your child's intelligence.

Husbands, wives and partners

Communication is the key for parents and partners to deal with the ongoing nature of dyslexia. It invariably falls on one parent or person in a partnership to be the leader of a support system for a child with dyslexia. If this is true of your family, the leader also needs to be a great communicator, ensuring that the other parent is kept up to date with all that is occurring in the life of the dyslexic child. Two heads are often better than one at finding solutions and two or more raving fans (passionate supporters) are what your child needs. If you are a single parent raising children on your own, you are already a one-person support network and an incredible hero in the eyes of most parents. Your immediate support network may be your direct family members, a best friend or a teacher, mentor or tutor who has a special relationship with your child. If you can't think of anyone special, remember that dyslexia is very common. Ask around, you will be amazed; there may be someone within your circle who knows more about dyslexia than you realise because they have it too.

Brothers and sisters

Brothers and sisters need to be brought into the fold to support their sibling with dyslexia. They will see first-hand the struggle that your child has every day at home and often at school too. You must educate them, and quickly. They need to understand why the struggle occurs and the impact it is having. It is important for any ridicule, teasing and put-downs from within your family to stop immediately if your child with dyslexia is going to remain confident or regain their confidence. Education at the appropriate age level is important, so explain your child's dyslexia to their brothers and sisters. It is also important to remind overly eager brothers and sisters not to start doing schoolwork, homework and reading on behalf of their dyslexic sibling.

Extended family and close family friends

The larger and more effective your support network is, the better for your child with dyslexia. When educating close family in particular, there will be some issues to overcome that may not be obvious straight away.

Firstly, you will have to deal with your family's preconceived ideas and personal views about what dyslexia is, and also their opinions on the impact it is having on your child and how it will impact on their future.

Secondly, you need to realise that when you formally bring to light your dyslexic child's condition, family members will react in many differing ways. There will be those who see it as a weakness and a slight on the family name. They may not want to talk about it, rather keep it hidden and downplay its significance. There are others who will be concerned about applying what they perceive as a label to a child and are concerned about the impact this may have on their future opportunities. For others, you may be detailing a dyslexic condition that they also struggled with in the past due to its genetic nature. These family members may be sympathetic and interested or based on their life experience, indicate to you that your child needs to toughen up and get over it, without all the fuss.

Families are often the hardest people to educate, because they believe they know us intimately, know what is best for us and will often not hesitate to tell us.

For example, your father may think your son has always been lazy and lacks motivation. Your sister may think you are overreacting and that there is nothing wrong with your son. You need to stand tall, wipe the slate clean, dispel all the myths and lay out the facts. You are the parent and you are in charge.

I find the best way to do this is to prepare family members mentally beforehand by informing them that you need to talk to them about something which is very serious. Make a time to sit down with them as you are going to be providing them with some important information that will impact upon the future of your child. When this get-together takes place, give them all the concrete evidence you have. Write the facts down with bullet points and give people a handout, so they have this for future reference. Make sure you include what is required of them and what you need them to do to help you and your child. I know this sounds so formal, but in many cases you will be seeking a change of attitude from people about your child and what is required from them in the form of support. If you take it seriously, family members will begin to understand the gravity of what you are asking of them.

Teachers and learning support specialists

Ongoing communication is the best way to ensure your child is receiving the best level of support at school. Provide teachers with all the information you have collected to date about your child. Let them know how your child with dyslexia learns, thinks, and feels. Ensure that communication lines are always open as discussed in Chapter 11.

Classmates and friends

A child who is good at everything is a rarity. Nearly all children understand what it feels like to struggle at something. This is part of growing up.

> **"Regardless of this fact, some children will make a habit of putting other children down, teasing and ridiculing them in an attempt to make themselves feel more powerful, when they themselves feel unsure or lack confidence."**

Being on the receiving end of this verbal harassment is not pleasant and it is possible your dyslexic child may be the recipient of this type of abuse as they struggle through school.

How To Help Your Child Develop A Strong Network Of Friends

Developing a strong network of friends is a good way to help your child to counteract this negative behaviour.

- Your child's strengths are a good place to start. If they are good at chess make sure they join the chess club, or if they are good at singing make sure they are in the school choir. Children will always look up to others who do things well.

- Inviting classmates over to play after school or on the weekend is another great way to help your child develop strong friendships outside the classroom environment.

- There is no doubt about it; playing team sports and being part of a club is also a great way for children to develop strong friendships. If your child is sporty, encourage them to get out there and have a go.

- If your child is being harassed at school, go and see the classroom teacher immediately. Nearly all teachers have a repertoire of classroom activities that can be implemented to reduce and combat the negative behaviour of children.

- Give your child the words to use to explain to their classmates how they learn differently. Children like to be informed and educated. For example, your child may say to a classmate, 'I read slower than you because I find it tricky to break down the words into smaller pieces. I understand what I read, I'm just slower. I'm great at maths though.' Or 'I have trouble remembering dates and facts because my brain doesn't store this information very well. I'm fine if I can write it down.'

- If children are encouraged to define themselves via their strengths and not their weaknesses, their positive outlook and their enthusiasm for life will soon help them to overcome and cope with the bad behaviour of others.

- As a family, if you are actively engaged in the school community you add another dimension to your child. Helping out in the classroom, coaching a sporting team, helping out on school excursions, all helps to encourage positive responses from other children towards your child.

The general community

Many people out in the community will be totally unaware of what having dyslexia will mean for your child. Some will always equate dyslexia with a lack of intelligence. If your child comes into constant contact with these people you will either need to seek to educate them or encourage your child to steer clear of them.

For the occasions where your child does have to put up with quizzical looks, intolerance, bullying or even pure contempt of their condition, you will need to provide them with the ability to provide answers, deal with their critics and hold their head up high. You can do this by giving them the words to say, if and when they are needed.

Chapter 17

How can I help my child to regain their confidence when they are already struggling at school and feel dumb and stupid?

How Children Define Themselves Is Critical To Their Self-Confidence

There is no doubt that a learning disability like dyslexia can create difficulties and challenges. Any parent of a truly dyslexic child will acknowledge this fact, but what is even more important is how your son or daughter defines him or herself.

Perhaps think about it like this: adults define themselves in many ways. This could include the school they went to, the job they have, the money they earn, the person they marry, the car they drive, the house and suburb they live in, the sport they play, their religion, the friends they have, the contribution they make to society or charity, and on and on it goes.

How do you define yourself? Think about it. If I asked your best friend to define you, would they give me the same answers? If I asked your son or daughter to define you or your mother or father, what would they say?

Generally, our self-confidence is directly linked to the way in which we define ourselves, and how we feel about it. Do we feel full of self-worth, worthless or somewhere in the middle? It is the same for our children.

The difference for a child with dyslexia is that their learning disability can become so dominant in their mind it can become the only way in which they define themselves.

Something like this:

> **"My name is John Brown and I have dyslexia. I can't read or write very well and I am not very good at school. I don't have many friends and nobody picks me for sport teams because they think I'm too dumb. I'm no good at anything. I get so frustrated and angry that I yell and scream a lot. My mum tries to help me, but she's got no idea, she just makes me do more schoolwork at home. I always get D's and E's on my report, even when I try. My teachers don't seem to care. What's the point? I hate my life."**

DyslexiaDaily.com

Now compare it to this.

> **"My name is Jack Smith and I have dyslexia. I have always had trouble reading and writing, but I go to learning support and it has made a huge difference. I am starting to improve, although I still have to try harder than everyone else. Now I can use a computer, I don't worry about my writing so much anymore. I just use my laptop. I am a real ideas person and I love doing science experiments, playing soccer and making things with my hands. I can remember lots of things in my head so the kids at school always ask me to remember answers to questions for them. I am going to be in the school play next year, because I'm good at learning my lines. My mum got a great computer program for me and now I am learning to spell better too. School is hard, but I have lots of friends and I enjoy it".**

What would your child say about themselves? How would they define themselves? In many cases, what a parent thinks is important a young child will think is important too. You are a very important key as to how your child defines themselves. Without realising it, what we as parents value highly, as time progresses, our children come to value too. Whether it is getting high academic grades at school, being good at sport, not swearing, and being respectful of others, making a contribution to others less fortunate or enjoying life and living it to the fullest.

After parents, the next most important influence on our young children is generally their teachers and their friends. Your child's teacher/s will spend between one hour per week and six hours per day with your child, depending on their school year level and their influence is enormous. How teachers respond to your child and their needs is critical to how your child will define themselves. When your child is struggling to read or to answer a question, will your child's teacher tap their foot impatiently with a grumpy face, or reassure your child and tell them to relax and take their time and have a go? Your child will know intuitively what their teachers think of them as a person and as a student and this attitude will in turn begin to reinforce how your child feels about themselves.

As our children move through the upper primary and into senior school, peers, friends and classmates will have even more influence. You can see this in the way children choose to wear their hair, what clothes they like to wear and the attitudes they develop to school, teachers, sport, music, television programs and so on. Your child will also be aware of what their peers think of them, again reinforcing their definition of themselves.

We all have a little voice inside our head that never stops chattering, our self-talk. This is based on how we define ourselves. It tends to say the same things to us over and over again. If it tells us we are hopeless and a failure, then that is invariably what we will be. If it tells us we are a success, then there is a good chance we will be. So how do we change the recorded message that keeps repeating in our child's brain, if it is a negative one?

Stop Focusing On Academic Results

Some parents get so caught up in their child's academic results that this is all they focus on. It becomes their one and only tool for measuring school success. Some parents will even provide monetary rewards based on the number of A's, B's and C's their children get on their school report. This will not work for your child if they are truly dyslexic. Rewards, bribes and threats are not the answer.

If effort was rewarded, maybe your child with dyslexia would receive all A's every time, because as you would recall brain scans generally show that a dyslexic brain is invariably working harder than that of a non-dyslexic brain to complete the same tasks. Your child needs to understand that your love and respect for them is not conditional based on their school report.

Your dyslexic child is operating within an education system that is based predominantly on books, reading, and writing and, in most cases, timed written exams. You need to be realistic about what your child is capable of achieving within the school environment. Try not to have unreal expectations and place extra undue pressure on your child. Every parent's expectations are different and by now you may be well aware of what your child is capable of. I always believe a mark of average C or 50-70% pass is exceptional for my children. For me it is all about my child passing each year level successfully and confidently. If my child gets a 'D' so be it. If they get a 'B' or 'A', they have more than exceeded my expectations. On the occasion where my child has received a 'D' or even an 'E', after further investigation and research I can usually put it down to the way in which an assessment or test was conducted, which obviously placed my child at a disadvantage because they have dyslexia.

Don't get me wrong, I still find this frustrating, but because I can justify the poor result and understand why it occurred, I can move on. When this occurs I use this situation to provide me with information to ensure if possible that appropriate assessments are provided in the future which do not disadvantage my child's learning style. You must always keep in mind that the assessment and reporting process in our schools does not provide you with a true reflection of your dyslexic child's intelligence.

I am not saying that academic results aren't important; they can be extremely important, particularly in the senior school years if your child has ambitions to go on to tertiary education. Many older students with dyslexia excel at higher education. It is important to understand that unless your child is feeling happy and confident at school, it will be extremely difficult for them to reach their full potential, so be realistic and nurture them through these challenging years. As they progress through the education system it will start to become obvious what their strengths and weaknesses are and how these can be used to help them to succeed in their senior high school years. The idea is to keep them happy and confident and feeling like a success in your eyes. Children hate to disappoint and you are their number one priority, so if you are happy, they will be too. The sense of security this provides can give your child the courage to overcome enormous obstacles.

Shift The Spotlight

A dyslexic child will often feel like a deer in the headlights of an oncoming car. Stuck in a moment in time, blinded by the fear and frustration of being dyslexic and unable to move forward, not knowing what is going to happen next.

It is our job as parents to take that spotlight off our children and to point it in another direction. Find, search and succeed at determining what they are good at... more than good at... great at.

Everybody has his or her area of expertise and your child is no different. Maybe your child already has a special talent and there is more than one area in which your child can excel. Perhaps their area of expertise is already identified, but they are too busy after school doing extra schoolwork and tutoring because they have fallen behind at school. Take the emphasis off school success and put it back on personal success.

> **"Your child can't be confident and successful until they understand how it feels to be confident and successful. It is your job to show them how it feels. Success breeds success. How many times have we heard that before?"**

Take the emphasis off success at school and find an alternative route to confidence and happiness. You will be amazed at how important this is. The way in which your child defines themselves will start to alter. As their confidence levels increase, it will start to spill over into other areas of their life including their confidence with their schoolwork and their success at school.

Focusing On One Burning Issue At A Time

Children are not adults, they don't think like adults, have the ability to manage themselves like adults or think on a big picture level. As adults we often forget this fact, assuming that our children are more capable of managing themselves than they really are. You know how we send them off to clean up their bedroom and they come back crying that they can't do it. In actual fact they made the mess and they can clean it up. The problem is they just don't know where to start.

The same is true for our child with a learning disability. They just don't know where to start to help themselves. We as their parents need to help them to find this place. In your child's mind dyslexia is just one great big enormous problem, which they have no idea how to tackle or fix. As adults we know the only way to tackle a big problem like this is logically with a step-by-step process.

The best place to start is at the beginning with your child's number one area of concern. We need to help them to identify their 'burning issue' and then work with them to overcome it, or to at least ease their burden and reduce the impact of this issue for them.

It is important to remember here that your number one burning issue of concern may not be the same as your child's. You might think the big problem is 'poor spelling' and if only that improved, your child's life and their school results would be much better. Maybe you are a good speller and you're sure you could offer first class assistance in this area, but spelling may not even feature in your child's mind as a burning issue. Instead for them it may be the fact that everyone in the class is calling them a dummy. If that is the case, you need to work on this burning issue for their sake. This exercise needs to be about what is bothering your child, not you. It is extremely important for your child's psychological welfare that they have some control over the management of their dyslexia and they can see by working at it with you that the future can begin to look a lot brighter.

Maybe you could try this. Sit down with them and ask them. 'What is the number one thing that bugs you about having dyslexia (or school) that you wish you could change tomorrow?'

They might know the answer immediately. They may say:

221

'I want to be able to read chapter books like everyone else'

'I can't write neatly'

'I don't know my times tables'

'The kids at school laugh at me and call me names'

'I don't have any friends and nobody lets me join in games at lunchtime'

Encourage them to be specific. 'I hate school' and 'learning to read sucks', are way too broad. Find out why they think that. Write all their answers down until you can help them to arrive at a specific reason.

Maybe they will know the one thing straight away; maybe they will give you 40 reasons off the top off their head. Write them all down. Now, your job is to identity their number one area of concern. Ask them to circle their top ten, then their top five and so on, until you identify their number one concern. Remember you want to find out their burning issue, not just the area of concern for that particular week.

If you have a child who is not capable of telling you what bothers them the most, you may need to make a qualified guess or ask the classroom teacher if they can help you to identify the biggest problem for your child to give you a place to start. Spending time in the classroom is also an option if you have the time available.

Once you have identified this 'burning issue' you have something to work with. Make it your number one priority to find ways to help your child to solve this problem. As parents, you may need to get creative to solve your child's problem, but as you do, you will start to see a change as they realise their struggle is manageable. Don't hesitate to ask for help from family members, teachers, sporting coaches, community groups and services.

If you tackle dyslexia one problem at a time, it does become manageable and the impact and changes become instantly apparent, especially to your child. Never give up, as there is a solution to every problem. As your child starts to recognise that there are solutions to their daily struggle, they will feel more in control of their destiny and their future. As you solve or ease one area of concern, identify the next and move on to solving or easing it. Working together with your child and easing their daily struggle is an empowering way to help maintain and increase their self-esteem and confidence.

Little Ears Are Always Listening

Having a child with dyslexia on top of everything else we as parents are facing today can be tough. It can present us with many varied and difficult challenges. As advocate, manager and supporter of our child with dyslexia, we often have to deal with what we see as ineffective teachers, a substandard education system and a society in general that does not seem to cater for dyslexic children. On days when this becomes apparent, it can make us want to whinge and complain and shout from the treetops how unfair it all is and how crazy it makes us feel, but... STOP RIGHT THERE.

When we as parents complain bitterly about all these things, we must remember that little dyslexic ears are listening. When we complain about our child's teacher, our partners, the system or any matter related to our children, our dyslexic child hears our words and takes them on board. Whether they are directly responsible for our rant or not, they may feel as though they are. After all, they may think you would not be complaining at all, if it weren't for the fact that they had dyslexia in the first place. Don't feel like you can never say anything negative or vent your frustrations, of course you can, but just avoid doing it when you are in listening range of your child with dyslexia. I can assure you they have enough negativity to overcome and deal with already without dealing with yours too.

Teach Your Child To Help Others Less Fortunate Than Themselves

It's amazing how our fears worries and concerns can be put back into perspective when we open our eyes and start to look around us. Yes, our child has dyslexia and yes, life can be hard and school challenging, but I can guarantee there are hundreds, thousands, even millions of people around us who are worse off. Your child is one of the lucky ones compared to so many. When the time is right, you need to remind your child of this fact.

Your child with dyslexia may not feel as though they have the emotional strength to focus their attention on others less fortunate than themselves, but it can be an important way of building their self-worth and self-confidence.

Telling them there are other people worse off than them is not enough. They will tell you that they know this is true, but will be so exhausted after a day at school that they may feel powerless to help and therefore become frustrated with you and shut you out. What they need is a call to action, which you may need to arrange. Don't just start donating to a charity – take your child and make a difference; help at a homeless shelter, spend time in an orphanage, go and volunteer at an aged care facility.

Helping others is a powerful medicine, it is rewarding and fulfilling. It can tap into your child's strengths, interests and talents as they provide assistance to others. This not only helps a great cause, it will provide your child with an injection of self-empowerment. Helping your child to help others can build good values and good character. This in turn can build their self-esteem and self-confidence, a great win/win scenario.

Help Your Child To Develop A Sense Of Humour

I put this last, not because it is the least important, but because when you have high levels of anxiety it is almost impossible to laugh except out of sheer nervous terror. I put it last because it is so important and I want you to be able to remember it.

When misfortune strikes, depending on our mood we can crumble into a heap on the floor, have a panic attack, die of embarrassment or have a good laugh. How we respond to our weaknesses can be a reflection of how we feel about ourselves. Everybody has weaknesses, no matter how perfect they appear; even Superman had kryptonite. It's how we allow our weaknesses to impact upon us that is important.

Having dyslexia can be extremely stressful; no one is going to disagree with me I'm sure. However if a child with dyslexia internalises the stress they feel every time their dyslexia reveals itself, the ramifications can be enormous on their health, happiness and well-being. There will be times when feeling stressed and anxious is unavoidable, like in the middle of a spelling test, but when the pressure is off, it is important to be able to smile or even laugh on occasion when dyslexia seems to jump out from no where.

I guess the message for you is to 'chill out' and 'lighten up'. This will allow your dyslexic child to follow suit. You need to follow this path yourself and set an example for your dyslexic child to follow. Make sure your child sees you laughing at your own misfortune from time to time, when you get lost, lose the car keys, don't get a joke or use the wrong word in a conversation.

Joel's Story As Told By Megan, His Mum

Sometimes when Joel my thirteen year old son is trying to tell me something that has happened which was extremely exciting, the words keep tripping out of his mouth. He uses lots of words like 'thingy's', 'stuff' and 'you know'. I try to remain serious, because I know what he is trying to tell me is important to him, but after a while when I have lost the thread of the conversation and have no idea what he is talking about, I can't help but smile without realising it. Often Joel will recognise this look and will try harder to find the right words. Usually this doesn't help and as he realises it, he starts to smile himself. It becomes a shared joke and he will fake indignation and pretend to walk away, saying. "You're just not that interested." After we have had a good laugh, the feeling of pressure and stress is reduced and we take the time to find the right words and get to the bottom of his important story.

I am not a perfect mother, although I try, Megan said, and there are times, when I can't help but be frustrated by his difficulty to find the right words, particularly when I am in a rush, dealing with another child or in the middle of doing something else, but that's life.

It is so important to teach your child to use laughter when appropriate as an effective strategy to deal with their dyslexia.

"As time goes by, your son or daughter will not remember you for how much money you spent. Their memories of childhood will linger on how much love, time and laughter you shared."

Chapter 18

A Resource list you need to know about

When you type the word 'dyslexia' into a computer search engine you are immediately bombarded with thousands of responses. You can spend hours sifting through them and not getting very far at all. Many are businesses trying to sell you tools for assessing and diagnosing dyslexia from the comfort of your own home. Others are selling teaching programs and learning resources, which you can buy in an attempt to help your child to overcome their learning disability and catch up at school.

You will read many websites and come away with one hundred definitions of dyslexia and no apparent solutions on how to help or get help for your struggling child. Every now and again you may get lucky and find a tool, a person or a resource which can be useful. However searching the internet can become an extremely time consuming, frustrating minefield when all you are really seeking is answers as to how you can help your struggling child and rebuild their self-confidence.

To make this journey easier for you, I have created a web based resource called DyslexiaDaily.com. It is a culmination of 12 years of research and includes all the tools and resources I wish I had when I began my journey to help and support my children with dyslexia.

Many world renowned experts contribute expertise and research to this website and post updates on a regular basis.

DyslexiaDaily.com Continues To Grow And Includes the following resources:

- Free eBooks
- Free articles
- Free posters
- Evidence based reading and spelling programs
- Books reviews
- A community forum
- A news blog
- The latest research
- Teaching and learning strategies

- Free teaching resources and aids
- Ideas for supporting children/students with dyslexia
- Information on related learning difficulties

On DyslexiaDaily.com you will find articles and free ebooks on topic such as;

- What is dyslexia?
- How to get an accurate diagnosis
- Signs and symptoms of dyslexia
- Dyslexia testing and assessment
- Dyslexia and school
- Dyslexia and teacher effectiveness
- Dyslexia research
- Tech tools and computers
- And much much more

A List of learning difficulties service providers

DyslexiaDaily.com also includes the only world-wide learning difficulties directory which is linked to Google maps, so you can search for service providers in your local area. DyslexiaDaily.com/ LearningDifficultiesDirectory, including:

- Dyslexia assessors
- Dyslexia associations
- Support groups
- Educational psychologists
- Developmental pediatricians
- Developmental optometrists and ophthalmologists
- Auditory processing specialists
- Dyslexia friendly/specialist schools
- Teacher training services

- Tutors
- Government dyslexia coordinators
- And lots more

If you know of a service provider who should be listed on this directory please tell them about it so they can submit their service for listing approval. They will find instructions on the website or alternatively you can let us know by going to the 'Contact Us' page at Dyslexiadaily.com

> **"Dyslexia Daily is a friendly on-line community where you'll meet like minded parents, educators and LD specialists to support you on your journey with dyslexia."**
>
> *Liz Dunoon*

Chapter 19

How to create an action plan

Getting Started-Create An Action Plan

Start supporting your child or student today.

Here's how to get started...

1. Start observing your child and making notes about their strengths and weaknesses.

2. Start collecting samples of your child schoolwork and items that demonstrate their strengths and weaknesses.

3. Talk to your child's school.

4. Get a notebook to keep track of any conversations, meetings and phone calls regarding your child. Include dates, who was present and the outcome.

5. Get a folder to keep copies of notes, letters, documents and school reports.

6. Have a professional diagnosis or assessment conducted. Ensure that the subsequent report is recognised by your local government education authority.

7. Make sure the school has a 'Support Plan' for your child that includes access to a support teacher for skills teaching and allows for accommodations in the classroom and for assessments.

8. Speak to the school regularly and check that teachers are aware of your child's report, support plan and learning needs. I recommend doing this at the beginning of every school term. Your aim is ensure their learning strengths are being utilised and their learning weaknesses supported.

For example you may ask:

- Whether you child is receiving small group support and how often?

- Is there minimal copying from the whiteboard?

- Are class notes provided in various formats?

DyslexiaDaily.com

- Is my child using a computer for writing or is a scribe provided?
- Can they use grid paper not lined, for Math?
- Are audio text and audio books available?
- Is there a multisensory literacy program?
- Is my child getting extra time for tests and exams?
- Are they allowed to give oral responses instead of writing when doing assessments?

The questions you ask should stem from your child's diagnostic report and from the support plan that has been created for them by the school.

9. Continue to maintain open lines of communication between your child, your school and yourself via email, phone or regular personal contact.

10. Find a good multisensory learning program that you can use at home to support what is being taught at school, or hire a specialist tutor.

11. Put a community support system in place for your child – consider immediate family, extended family and friends, your child's friends, teachers and local community groups.

12. Put strategies in place to maintain and build your child's self esteem and confidence. Allow them to focus on their areas of interest and strength.

You can find a downloadable copy of this *Parent Action Plan* under Free Resources at **DyslexiaDaily.com**.

Preparing For A New Year At School

The holidays are coming to an end and you begin to notice that your child is becoming anxious, stressed, grumpy, not eating or losing sleep. What's going on? Then it hits you that the commencement of the new school year is looming and your child is starting to stress, big time. New teachers, harder schoolwork, more of it, homework and increasing academic expectations. This can be a stressful time for all children, but particularly for a child with dyslexia.

My final tip is a simple but incredibly effective strategy that can help to alleviate this starting back to school anxiety. In fact it can completely change your child's school year and their learning outcomes. If you do nothing else after reading this book – Please do this.

Create a simple statement of your child's abilities for every teacher that will come in contact with your child throughout the coming year. Include:

1. My child's learning strengths.

2. My child's learning weaknesses.

3. How my child likes to learn.

Even better get them to help you to write it. This document only needs to be one or two sheets of paper that the teacher can print out and refer to.

That's it, plain and simple. Every year I email this to my children's new teachers, both classroom and specialist subject teachers, and every year the teachers email me back their thanks. Now they know how to start the year off in a positive and proactive way and get the best from my child from day one. This is a simple, but powerful strategy and well worth the 20 minutes or so it will take you to write it.

Your child's teacher is faced with 20-30 new students in every class as the new school year commences. If you were in their position wouldn't you want to know how best to reach and teach them effectively?

You can find a downloadable copy of this *New School Year Student Statement* under Free Resources on **DyslexiaDaily.com** for you to simply fill out.

Liz and Andrew Dunoon

Above all, believe in your child and tell them constantly that you do, because with your love and ongoing support they can and will be a success.

"I wish you and your family happiness, good health and future personal success"

Liz Dunoon